The Time of Our Lives

Other books by Robert Dessaix
available from Brio

A Mother's Disgrace
Arabesques
Corfu
Night Letters
Twilight of Love

The Time of Our Lives

Growing older well

Robert Dessaix

b
BRIO

BRIO

First published by Brio in 2020

Brio Books Pty Ltd
PO Box Q324, QVB Post Office,
NSW 1230, Australia

briobooks.com.au

All rights reserved. Without limiting the rights under copyright below, no part of this publication shall be reproduced, stored in or introduced into a retrieval system, or transmitted in any form or by any means (electronic, mechanical, photocopying, recording or otherwise), without the prior permission of both the copyright holder and the publisher.

The moral right of the author has been asserted.

Text copyright © Robert Dessaix 2020

ISBN 9781922267481 (Paperback)

'Why All the Embarrassment About Being Happy' from *The Peace of Wild Things: And Other Poems* by Wendall Berry © 1964 published by Penguin Books. Reproduced by permission of Penguin Books Ltd. © 2018

'The City' from *C. P. CAVAFY: Collected Poems, Revised Edition* translated by Edmund Keeley and Philip Sherrard, ed. by George Savidis. Translation copyright © 1975, 1992 by Edmund Keeley and Philip Sherrard. Reprinted by permission of Princeton University Press."

Cover and internal design and typesetting copyright © Brio Books 2020
Cover design by Brio Books, briobooks.com.au
Author photograph: Matthew Venables

Papers used by Brio Books are natural, recyclable products made from wood grown in sustainable forests. The manufacturing processes conform to the environmental regulations of the country of origin.

PART I

'The last enemy …'
(I Corinthians 15)

Forever Young

*I*tchi gitchi ya ya da da ... (now we're pumping) ... getcha getcha ya ya here ... You betcha! Across the lawn from me in the sun, a bunch of hotel guests with their wellness instructor were prancing, swivelling to the music, brown limbs gleaming, boom box thumping by the lotus pond ... *Voulez-vous coucher avec moi ce soir? Voulez-vous coucher avec moi?*

'Sure, sashay right over, why don't you?' I thought to myself as I eyed this perky performance from the divan in the hotel's garden pavilion. I felt all jazzed up just watching. At that moment I'd have *coucher*'d with practically anyone. Every morning that week, soon after sunrise, the young Balinese guy, Budi, had been strutting his stuff here in time to the music, bare-legged, sweaty singlet sticking to his chest, with a few middle-aged guests gyrating along beside him, punching the air. Against the fall of ruby-red flowers on the coral vine, it was a mesmerising sight. I wasn't tempted to join in, though—well, a little, perhaps, synchronised dancing is always seductive, but I know my limits. Apparently there's nothing like energetic dance movements to boost the cognitive functions—or so a nice Englishman in glasses claimed on television recently. Something about synaptic firing, as I remember.

Some days, though, cognitive functions just aren't the priority. It was all very mind-body, Budi's class, which can be quite cheering when you're twenty-five and still looking good in shorts, as Budi was, especially now the soul is out of fashion. It may lose its appeal when Alzheimer's and peripheral neuropathy kick in, but right there at that moment it was very much the *plat du jour*. There was something about it that reminded me of the Greeks: the smooth, slender, Greek ideal of strong-shouldered beauty, male and female, has more or less taken over the world now—not the actual world, obviously, but minds from Montreal to Melbourne. Even in Mumbai I noticed that the billboards all over the city featured gods and goddesses in the Greek mould, not the Indians you see in the streets or hanging out of buses.

All the same, I was aware as I sat there in that hotel garden outside Yogyakarta that this display of jerking, jiving, jumping bodies, while entertaining and exhilarating, was also at some deeper level unsettling. Yet what on Earth could have been unsettling about such innocent calisthenics? Everyone was clearly right into it, after all. It looked sexy, it looked enlivening, it looked *fun*. They were publicly thumbing their noses at conventional ideas about what sort of behaviour was seemly at a certain age, and particularly about how an ageing body should display its pale, wrinkled self in public. And who doesn't get a kick out of doing that? Needless to say, like mindfulness and Tibetan singing-bowl sessions, these kinds of classes are a clear class-signifier for us—this whole hotel is a class-signifier, for that matter, as are my shoes and the Brazilian maca-root shaving cream I favour—but that's not what unsettles me.

Renate, for instance, who was well into her sixties, was electrified, she was reborn, it was never like this in Utrecht before breakfast on a Thursday; Malcolm from Melbourne was hovering between euphoria and panic, as dancers often do, amazed to find he had it in him to caper like this in public, yet at the same time unnerved, like a hang-glider coming in to land; while the couple from Kuala Lumpur were literally in an altered state, they were not just *spry* any more, they really were kids at play again, a little bewildered, but youthfully loose-limbed, bursting with energy—for now, at least.

I was bothered, however slightly, for the same reason I'm bothered by gyms, I suspect, not to mention joggers. Neither gyms nor joggers disturb me *deeply*—I'd like that to be unequivocally clear from the start—I don't think they should be banned. Even with reasonably good health and a mind in working order, it's hard to grow old well. Round and round we go, in ever-tightening circles, like water down a plug-hole, and then we're gone. So how you deal with your body's gradual collapse is your business, not mine. All the same, something about these regimens does cause unease. Years ago, I recall, when I was a regular at a gym near my house, something would put me on edge as soon as I pushed open the door. There was always a kind of tense self-consciousness in the air, even when there was almost nobody there. Everyone without exception—the women with blonde ponytails pounding away on the treadmill, going nowhere, the swimmers doing lap after lap in the pool, the young men lifting weights, biceps straining, the fit, the unfit, the taut, the sagging, the aged, the youthful, *everybody* performing these rituals—looked anxious. Each and every one of them gave the impression of fighting a losing battle while pretending to have the upper hand. Against what, though? What were they fighting against? Flabbiness? Obesity? Heart disease? Stress? What?

'Death, of course,' said my friend Sarah next morning without a moment's hesitation when I asked her what she thought all the joggers and gymnasts were trying to hold at bay. 'What else? It's death they're afraid of—or at least dying.' She gave me a slightly lop-sided smile, not being in her prime any more, and cast a wry Hungarian eye over that morning's group performing its synchronised moves by the pond. 'This lot is still just young enough to imagine it can win.' She laughed in that throaty way only smokers can. She was looking more and more like

Maggie Smith that winter, as a host of women of a certain class eventually do.

'Perhaps they just want to stay limber.'

'Limber?' Sarah sometimes likes to savour a word as if hearing it for the first time. In reality, like so many Hungarians, she speaks English better than the rest of us. 'Limber is always good, of *course*. Covers a host of sins.'

'And lithe,' I said. I'm a fan of lithe. Freddie Mercury was lithe. (And Zoroastrian, too, from Zanzibar ... but my mind was wandering.)

'Still, at root,' she said, eyes fixed on the group gyrating in the sun, 'I think they simply want to avoid getting old. And facing what comes next. I can't say I blame them—at their age.'

'But you can't win at that game, can you.'

'No, it's quite futile.'

'None of it works,' I mumbled, half under my breath. 'Time passes and things fall apart.' I studied the merrily cavorting crew, all gleaming in the sun. 'In the end *their* brains will liquefy and dribble out of their mouths and ears just like everyone else's.'

'I suppose they will.' At our advanced age this thought does not unduly alarm us. It doesn't alarm the young much, either, because it's all so notional, but it frightens the hell out of the middle-aged.

'Not everyone thinks it will end badly, though, do they.'

'Who, for example?'

'Americans, for a start,' I said. 'Americans seem to have an inborn predilection for happy endings. They confuse life with *Singin' in the Rain*. Everything's going to be *just fine*.'

The beat was from 'Stayin' Alive' that morning, and Budi, a mere stone's throw away across the grass in his knee-length blue shorts, was our dancin' man—breakin' and shakin' and stayin' fetchingly alive. He was drilling his squad of foreigners to fantasise about being as loose-limbed and fit as he was. *Ah ha ha ha, stayin' alive, stayin' alive.* (*Saturday Night Fever*, I admit, ends fairly bleakly: moving to Manhattan is not my idea of a happy ending. All the same, I have a point about Americans.)

'It's like taking the waters, really, don't you think?' I said after a few moments. 'Remember that fad?'

'I'm from Budapest, darling. We had the best bathing establishments in Europe. It wasn't just a fad.'

'People aren't still doing it, surely, are they?'

'By the thousand! But they call it something else these days. You don't "take the waters" now, you pamper yourself at ... what do they call it? Ah, yes—a wellness spa.'

'Well, I doubt anyone ever lived a second longer for lolling in a wellness spa.'

'Maybe not, but in trying to, people ...' She waved one hand in the air. A tiny gem on her ring flashed blue in the sun.

'What?'

'Oh, I don't know—people enjoy their bodies in these places, openly, publicly, extravagantly. They feel beautiful, they feel chic ... a touch decadent, perhaps, in a faintly Roman sort of way, if you know what I mean.'

I've never felt comfortable with that sort of thing, to be frank—luxuriating in your body in public—try as I might to loosen up a bit about it. I just never have. Much too sincerely carnal. That said, I have no objection to it in the theatre.

'What you obviously *can* do, though, is stave off *looking* old,' Sarah went on, her eyes still fixed on the exercise class. She hadn't much bothered to stave off anything herself—a thin *couche* each morning of some special *anti-rides* unguent, because one wants to give the impression one looks after oneself, but nothing more than that. Her face looked like what it was: the face of a woman who had lived a long, rich life—a difficult one in recent years—and lived it intensely, eyes wide open. In other words, a 'finely seasoned face', to quote Daniel Klein's lively musings on ageing in his *Travels with Epicurus*. 'The face is me,' he says, 'it's my life.' So why would you stretch and paint over it? 'Speaking of which,' Sarah said, 'Jane Fonda's picture was in the paper the other day—did you see it? She's older than we are but looks thirty-two.'

'But what's the point of that sort of thing, really? All that maintenance—for what? You're still rotting away inside.'

'I think we know perfectly well what the point is.' Did we? 'To stay attractive. You can't cheat death, but you can stay attractive.'

'Do you mean sexually?'

'*Obviously* I mean sexually. Why else would you get a facelift?'

'You mean looking twenty-five when you're seventy-five might spice up your sex life a bit?'

'Well, it won't hurt, will it.'

'What are the figures on this, I wonder? Does anyone know?'

'At their age,' Sarah said, nodding at our younger fellow guests, 'you still think it's worth giving it a shot. That's one good thing about being *actually* old, in my opinion: it finally dawns on you that there's no longer any point at all in faking youth. You look like shit and will soon be dead. You can relax.' Another throaty laugh. I'd known Sarah since the age of ten and she'd never been a romantic. We sat for a moment, engrossed in the show across the lawn. 'Were you ever in love with John Travolta, by the way?'

'I don't remember,' I said, recalling very clearly the dark-haired figure in the white suit, stabbing at the air. 'It was so long ago.'

'I don't believe you. I was.'

'Really? But you …'

'I was always willing to make an exception for John Travolta.' She paused to take a last sip of tea. 'Are you afraid of death, do you think?'

I had to chuckle: very few friends will put a question like this to you over breakfast. 'Hardly at all these days, no—well, not of being dead, if that's what you mean.'

'Nor am I. Not of *being* dead.'

Strange to relate, in later life there doesn't seem to me to be much point in spending time on that. Flicking through a Melbourne newspaper on the plane the other day I lit upon a piece by a young journalist I like (with a cheeky Polish name and spectacles) in which he wrote he thought that, as free-thinking 'baby-boomers' approached death, the churches might fill up again. How off-putting, whether it's true or false, but I think it's a much younger man's take on things. As death's door creaks open, something unexpected happens.

For the first time in years a vivid picture of a friend called David Fosse flashed into my mind: emaciated and blind, he lay dying in a Sydney hospice with just a few weeks left. It was the mid-eighties and he was the first close friend of mine to die of AIDS. His family, being devoutly Christian, had disowned him, so he lay there for the most part totally alone for those days he knew were his last. Was he afraid? Not at all. 'What of?' was all he said when I asked him. Distressed and regretful, but not afraid. And how did he spend his time? Listening to talking books—tapes of novels by Dickens and Thackeray. Beauty. What he wanted was beauty, that's all. And wit, of course. And language—that goes without saying. And the sense of a gentle heart beholding him. (You can't really say that in English, I know, but that's what he wanted.)

'Yes, you can try to *look* young forever,' Sarah went on, 'like Jane Fonda and whatshername from … you know …'

'Joanna Lumley.'

'It's the names that go first, isn't it. Nouns come next, apparently. Yes, her. You can try to die young as late as possible, in other words…'

'Did you just make that up?'

'No. Or you can do what you've done.'

'What's that?'

'Fail to grow up in the first place.'

'I see,' I said, but didn't—not at that moment.

I'd have pursued the question, but, once Budi, Renate, Malcolm and the rest had dispersed sweatily, wandering off to shower and breakfast, Sarah asked me to walk with her to her room. She has a cane to help her negotiate the slippery stone floors, but all I really had to do was to take her elbow as we went up steps, and there weren't many of those because it was just a scattering of renovated houses and pavilions, this hotel, spanning the village street amongst the bamboo, the coconut palms and the lush, dangling ferns. Such a wonderful place to do nothing in—a pretend Javanese village, sunk in a paradise of ponds and tumbling greenery, with white stone buddhas in nooks left over from the days when Buddhists lived here. Tomorrow would be a big day—Borobudur (speaking of both buddhas and steps)—and Sarah had to rest up for it. Borobudur is a stupa the size of a hill. It's vital to climb to the top.

'I'll climb as far as I feel like climbing,' Sarah replied when I told her, 'and not an inch more. See you at lunch.'

What Are We Afraid Of, Really?

Could it be true that we try to stay young in the way we look in the hope of putting off being dead or, at the very least, dying? Is that really why we do it (if we do)? Are all those youth-enhancing hormone treatments, facelifts and injections, all those yoga and tai chi regimens, all that jogging, all those punishing diets, the implants and anti-ageing serums, all that time-consuming *upkeep*—is it all in reality, at least subconsciously, just a self-deluding stratagem to postpone what we fear above all things: death? There must be more to it than that, surely. You don't spend half your life on maintenance of one kind or another just to hoodwink death. Or do you?

After seeing Sarah to her room to rest on her terrace with a book, I set off on a slow stroll through the *kampung*—the village the hotel is nestled in—gathering my thoughts. It's not one of those Javanese villages lost in some remote valley, looking much as it did when the Dutch arrived, but a busy outer-urban *kampung* with its network of small houses and gardens and chickens, its cemeteries and mosques (just two), its schools, its tea shops and corner stalls, squeezed between the main road south from the city proper and the rice-fields. It's not postcard pretty, the houses being mostly too run-down for that, and some American visitors have even complained to Reception about the poverty on their doorstep, apparently, but for me it's a pleasure to wander alone around its quiet laneways, especially in the morning cool or at dusk. Everyone whose eye I catch nods, many smile, and there are few vehicles, for the most part just push-bikes and motor-scooters. Many bodies here are bent with age, many faces weathered, even ancient. Of course, in an Indonesian village the immensely elderly for the most part do not venture out. (Indeed, in some parts of Indonesia, such as Bali, if they are not just decrepit but also demented, they are caged or kept in stocks in the backyard. Respect does not imply a commitment to aged care.)

Quite a few well-known thinkers seem to agree with Sarah that pretty well everything we do is indeed a ploy to deny death. Epicurus, for instance, over two millennia ago in Athens, thought the denial of death responsible for most of our neuroses and our obsession with our own wellbeing. What was there to fear? Death as the end? Concentrate instead, he said, on close friendships, self-sufficiency and thoughtful tranquillity. I've never seen the point of tranquillity, I must say—give me animation any day—but I don't live in ancient Athens. In any case, the whole world dreams of it constantly. To be busy all day and then expensively tranquil for an hour or two is our ideal these days. The fantasy smells of Los Angeles. I see men and women walking fast, talking fast, arguing loudly, as Americans do, and then chilling out in a watery spa with floating candles. For the cultural anthropologist Ernest Becker, for instance, from the moment we first realise it's not Disneyland out there beyond the front gate, as we'd naïvely thought (until Mother told us where sausages come from or the cat got run over), but a terrifying slaughterhouse—every square inch of the planet, every drop of water a killing field, never mind about Cambodia—our human experience becomes one long 'immortality project', doomed from the start. After all, entropy can't be argued with—you're falling apart physically and *there* you go. So, to stare down death and reach for immortality, humans typically don't just resort to keeping the body in shape, as we might have expected, but also, according to Becker in *The Denial of Death*, to various ingenious symbolic systems.

There's nothing humans like more than a system. To this day they even think of themselves as systems (rather than as two-legged biological battlefields). Typically, most humans yearn for systems that are much bigger and longer-lasting than they are themselves, such as the Communist Party, say, the House of Islam, America or even Gaia, striving to merge with one or more of them. Some, more modestly, consider themselves to be members of a 'community', one that looks good for the long-term, if not eternity (the Aboriginal, Esperanto, LGBTQIA+ or rugby community—the list is long). Failing those sorts of systems, almost everyone at least has the family. Loners everywhere arouse suspicion.

If Becker is to be believed, many of us also take refuge in hero figures in order to do battle with mortality. Heroes fight. There's something timeless about heroes, whatever their fate in reality. There are the countless war heroes we swear never to forget, for instance, although we quickly do. In the local park where I walk my dog, there stands in splendid isolation a grey slab with LEST WE FORGET carved into it. There are no names. We are supposed to hold our dead warriors in our hearts eternally, yet who can remember a single name apart from one grandfather's and the odd general's? On the other hand, mention Achilles or Spartacus or Joan of Arc to any of the dog-walkers in the park and time will evaporate. In the old Soviet Union, now I come to think of it, statues of heroes (and some heroines) were everywhere: in a culture where death's finality was official, you needed them to distract you from the brutishness of now. The heroes were stony-faced, muscular, abstracted and ubiquitous. From beyond time.

There are the sporting heroes, too, particularly amongst the players of the more warlike games, who are distinct from mere athletes of the hurdling, cycling or tennis-playing kind. Consequently, in our society anything that saps the martial spirit is frowned upon or suppressed—the more refined pleasures, the cult of beauty, anything that might lift them above brute matter, whatever is thought to be *halus* about a man or woman, as the Javanese might think of it. (In one word, if holding one word in your mind would help: silk. Think of silk. We're suspicious of men in silk. Silk, as the Romans remarked more than once, *unmans*—at least from a Western perspective. Perhaps this is why so many of us prize it, but that's another matter entirely. In Java, though, kings have been wearing silk batik for a thousand years. There was nothing unmanly about Javanese kings.)

When a sporting hero actually dies, as a well-known golfer did not long ago before growing old, the public is not just saddened but utterly forsaken. Every now and again the nation is shocked by the untimely death of a sportsman. The show is suddenly over, as it were. The house-lights have gone up and the music has died. Time to go home. Heroes can't really save us from what's waiting for us there.

There's cultural fame as well, of course, which need not be quite so explicitly linked to crushing a foe as the heroic sporting feats are. Lady Gaga isn't crushing anybody—or not at least in an Alexander the Great sense. In the intricate symbolic systems of both high art and popular culture, the megastars function as gods and goddesses, exactly like the characters from the *Ramayana*. Flawed, but divine. Recognisably human, yet, like Rama or Osiris, flourishing in another dimension. Not tediously immortal like the Virgin Mary, but seemingly outside time—for the moment, at any rate. London's National Portrait Gallery is stuffed full of pictures of these exalted beings, from Tudor kings to Margaret Drabble and David Bowie. You feel magnified to your very core—indeed, *in* your very core—as soon as you walk in the door of the National Portrait Gallery, you feel vast, ageless, rooted in a panoply of greatness that's never-ending (and if you're even remotely British, it's *your* panoply)—all the while being absolutely nobody yourself, nobody at all. It may be an illusion, but it's a momentarily transfiguring one: a snook has indeed been cocked at death. I wouldn't dream of going to London without spending at least an hour or two in the National Portrait Gallery.

Institutional religion is the perfect symbolic system,

however, the system outperforming all other systems, for combatting death: everything from the Russian Orthodox Church to the Moonies dresses itself up as eternal while at the same time promising everlasting life to the symbol-juggling faithful on a different, for the moment invisible and unreachable, plane altogether. Should either claim prove to have been bogus, the institution will be in the clear: you'll be well and truly dead. It doesn't get much better than that!

A quick stroll up the Grand Colonnade in Palmyra can be sobering in this regard—or it used to be before Muslim extremists got to it—as I found a few years ago just as Syria was about to fall apart: you pass the ruins of dozens of temples and sanctuaries dedicated to deities whose names mean little or nothing to anyone any more—Bel, Baalshamin, Durahlun, Nebu, Yarhibol, Yaglibol, Nanai, Herta, the Arab goddess Allat and a host of others. All gone. As dead as Isis. Syllables referring to nothing. However, despite the rumours that abound in tertiary institutions across the planet, religion itself is flourishing as never before. Who'd have thought? In my experience as a life-long traveller, most of the planet is still wildly animated by religion. It's not so much the case in the café-dotted bits of it where the well-fed, well-read, thinking classes graze (my own crowd, actually, as well as my journalist friend's—the man with the Polish name at the Melbourne *Age*). In Fitzroy, say, or Islington in London, most have lost their confidence in religious dogma, and so, like an overvalued currency it's collapsing fast there, but, to my eyes, the bulk of humanity still wants to find an authoritative way to transcend this brutally random universe while simultaneously loving it. Even in the West, vast numbers of thinking people tolerate remnants of religion in their lives in the hope, as John Updike once remarked, that it will allow them to ignore nothingness while they get on with 'the jobs of life' (adultery and so on, presumably, if his fiction is anything to go by). So Nietzsche spoke too soon, I think.

Religion may be just mumbo-jumbo, but, importantly, it's solemnised mumbo-jumbo—that's the thing. It's play of the most sophisticated kind and we all love to play. Take Shiva's nightly putting-to-bed ritual in the Meenakshi Temple in Madurai: a stone idol is borne in a silver palanquin by priests stripped to the waist, gleaming in the firelight, into the temple's forbidden heart where his wife Parvati awaits him in their bed chamber. It's noisy, full of light and vibrant colours and dancing bodies and joy. 'Do you really believe that Parvati is waiting for Shiva to come to her in there tonight?' I asked my guide. He guffawed. Clearly my naïvety tickled him.

'That's a Western question,' he said, and would say no more. We Westerners are so hung up on truth. We would do well to play more.

Over and above these various types of symbolic systems, there is also the rather piffling kind of immortality promised by becoming one day a part of nature (speaking of things bigger than yourself). 'I love to think,' a friend of mine said recently when the subject of cremation popped up over lunch, 'of merging with the Earth one day, of being reborn as … oh I don't know … a tree or a sea-anemone.' What is there to love about this? She must be desperate. What has a sea-anemone or lump of wombat poo got to do with immortality? In a similar vein, some artists seek comfort in the idea that their art will live on 'forever', meaning, presumably, at least until their grandchildren are dead. This is blather. As Woody Allen once remarked apropos of this kind of tosh, 'I don't want to achieve immortality through my work, I want to achieve it through not dying.' Precisely. Tolstoy, whose ego was even more voluminous than Allen's, said much the same thing: the only kind of immortality he was interested in was being Leo Tolstoy forever. It's what most religions (although not all) wisely promise to deliver. As luck would have it, delivery can't be tracked.

In Silicon Valley the hunt is apparently on for a physical 'solution to death', which is now seen as a biotechnical problem. The geeks at Google are going to cure death, it's believed, thwarting the grim reaper and making it possible to live *here* forever. In some medical circles it's currently hoped that by eradicating the fried-egg-shaped 'senescent cells' in our bodies that 'drive the ageing process and diseases', science might eventually banish dying altogether. I find this thought truly terrifying. Death, as Martine Rothblatt, celebrity founder of the biotechnology company United Therapeutics, has phrased it, might well become optional. Martine Rothblatt lives in style in Florida, so I'm not sure she quite understands the ramifications of what she's saying. Like a lot of people in Florida, she doesn't like the whole death thing. She's taken with the idea of release from the cycle of death and rebirth, but not in a Hindu or Buddhist way. Instead of oneness with the One Supreme Self, it's all nematode worms and glutathione these days in Florida. Who, you might wonder, would want to live literally forever here on this planet? Especially in Florida. Has Martine Rothblatt thought this through?

At the edge of the *kampung*, where I had ended up ruminating alone on all these things that morning after taking Sarah to her room, the sweet lushness of the rice paddies I'd first glimpsed amongst the trunks of the coconut palms opened up before me and stretched yellow and green to the line of hills in the east. Some buzzing motor-scooters in the distance, a minaret or two, a buffalo, boys fishing in the stream. All the people who'd crossed my path that morning would likely have seen their lives as strands in two vast symbolic tapestries of meaning, exactly as their ancestors had: firstly, in the abode of Islam, the Dar-al-Islam, encircling the globe; and secondly, in their family, life without a family being unimaginable in Java. Your family stretches backwards into antiquity, a system of interlocking stories and myths giving substance to everything you do, and forwards into a limitless, living web of meaning. This grandfather selling soap and cigarettes in the stall on the corner near the mosque was part of a network of beings that would last forever and meet again in paradise, as was every child playing in the dusty schoolyard, every farmer planting rice in the fields behind the hotel, every mother hanging out the day's washing on her porch. And the family was woven into the village and the village into the sultanate and the sultanate into Java and so on without end. What must it be like to have a family? I've heard all the words for what it's like, naturally—nobody speaks or writes a word these days without mentioning their family—but I still can't easily imagine the feeling of having one. Deep down I'm suspicious of families. Mine evaporated very early on. I am richly companioned, and there's always a dog, but that's not the same thing at all. That's not a system.

Just across the fields where the city itself begins (the roaring, screeching, grinding city, teeming just over there, behind that line of trees), there are pockets where it's a little different, naturally, but in the Javanese countryside time is a great frothing whirl of things you tumble about in, clinging onto those two ropes:

religion and family. Your time there, outside the city, is never your own, that's the point. At set times the five calls to prayer break up your day, and Ramadan breaks up your year according to the Islamic calendar, in a way completely beyond your control. For centuries the Javanese have also had their own five-day week, the *pasaran*, for their ritual cycles, not to mention numerous auspicious days—the day a saint allegedly died, for instance. In the boundless turbulence of living, as you flap about in the currents, you cling to whatever gives you a sense of rootedness—what else can you do? That's your way of being in the world. And so you always seem to be running late. At half past seven you wash up where you were meant to be at six. Interestingly, you also have little sense of leisure in the modern meaning of the word, because to be leisured is to be master of your own time. And that's something you rarely are in Java—unoccupied sometimes, but hardly at leisure. In the city, however, beyond the line of trees, some Javanese are flapping about in the time-swirl less, doing things by the clock these days, even exploring what leisure means. Just like us. At long last, even here in Central Java, there's something to move forward towards: finally, for many Javanese time is money rather than experience.

At leisure myself that morning, I perched for a moment on a low wall beside the stream that waters the paddy fields to breathe in the earthy warmth and let my mind wander, but it didn't wander, it flew instantly back home to St Ursula's. I had to face up to what had happened at St Ursula's.

Rita's Room

A week before I left for Java, Rita fell over again. On her face. At St Ursula's, just over the hill from where we live. 'Hullo, Rita!' I say brightly when I get to her bedside, taking her hand. We let our clasped hands lie on the bed-cover. I gently stroke her papery skin. She's shadow-puppet thin.

'Where's the other one, Olive?' she mumbles. She always calls me 'Olive' these days.

'Coming,' I say, smiling witlessly, although she's the one who's lost her mind. 'But here's Polly to see you.' The dog is feeling edgy, though, and tries to leave. The dog doesn't like endings. She likes beginnings.

'Where's the other one?'

'Coming. He'll be here in a minute.'

'Sink?'

'In a minute. Soon.'

'Can I go home now, Olive?'

'Not quite yet.' Olive was her best friend back at the Village, where she spent the last twenty years or so until she fell over and ended up here at the Grange. Montpellier Gardens, the Village was called. Like the Holy Roman Empire, which wasn't holy, Roman or an empire, Montpellier Gardens wasn't a village, had no gardens and nothing to do with the south of France. Between the slats in the venetians I can see outside, but it's dispiriting. Geraniums in pots around a concrete inner courtyard. They need watering.

'Mngk,' she says. The bruise on her cheek is a delicate mauve.

'Yes.'

So far so good. We're still here together. It's an intensely emotional moment, naturally, sad in a way that's hard to find the right words for—I feel scooped out, I feel impotent, I want to sob—but I'm not exactly *unhappy*.

Rita says 'mngk' again, dribbles a bit and closes her eyes. Rita is old, catastrophically old, remembering almost nothing. Even looking backwards is now beyond her. Rita, as the nurse has explained, is shutting down. The nurses here are so bracingly unsentimental. They're impossible to rattle. On the wall above Rita's bed is a small cross—there's no Jesus nailed to it, it's just a spindly wooden cross, hinting vaguely at a life to come. Rita, as far as I know, has never had a religious thought in her life, unless you count sending out Christmas cards, which I don't. Remembering nothing, Rita now foresees almost nothing, either. However, this *is*, after all, the Grange at St Ursula's. Crosses are to be expected. I don't trust the word 'grange', to be frank. It used to smell of … oh, I don't know … horse manure, not to put too fine a point on it, but also hay, oats, the sorts of things an abbot or lord of the manor might have wanted to store in a building out the back. ('Manor'—there's another one.) Now look what it means.

She does remember her son, though, and seems distressed that he's not here with me. When he comes in—where can he be, for goodness' sake, and why is he taking so long?—she'll smile. That's all that's left now, to be honest—this wordless welling-up of tenderness towards her son. And the dog.

When Peter finally does arrive a few minutes later, I

pass him his mother's mottled hand and step outside to compose myself a little. I head for the garden at the back. The gaunt figure in the bed in the room beside Rita's is calling out hoarsely: 'Somebody help me, somebody help me, somebody help me, somebody help me …' Nobody even hears her any more. The carer who passes me in the corridor outside her room beams at me and walks briskly on. The cries are white noise. I understand.

Out in the damp garden amongst the ferns and candy-pink azaleas, my mind starts slowly spiralling upwards into the light. Round and round it goes, up and around, looping higher and higher, singing thinly like a flute at the top of my white-haired head—my still bright-eyed yet startlingly white-haired head. (To this day I can't quite believe how white it is when I catch sight of it in the mirror. You can see my head from half a block away.) Why, I wonder, am I not unhappy?

Ashamed though I am to admit it, I suspect I have a secret knack for a kind of common or garden-variety happiness, or at least for holding onto it when it strikes. Not for jubilation, which is something I lack all talent for, nor exuberance or crowing with joy or anything cock-a-hoop, but for a kind of buoyancy. Only a

Broadway musical (*Cabaret*, say, or *Chicago*) can make me positively exultant, although watching the prancing Freddie Mercury belt out '*Mama* …' at the Live Aid concert in London that summer evening in 1985 (on YouTube, I wasn't there) is electrifyingly beautiful as well. On reflection, when that young Kazakh, Dimash Kudaibergen, hit the high notes on *America's Got Talent* a year or two ago, I also became instantly tearful, just like one of the judges, Britney Spears (whose name is an anagram for Presbyterian, which always cheers me up immensely). My mind was gently ravished by the Kazakh's piercing delicacy, I was left febrile in its wake. It's spine-chilling, this kind of rarefied joy, even Beethoven rarely transports me to quite those heights. For the most part, however, I simply have a flair for a sort of intensely felt contentment. Why should I be ashamed?

'Why all the embarrassment about being happy?' Wendell Berry asked many years ago. I don't know much about Wendell Berry, but I do know he's old, much older than I am, and a farmer and a poet, if I'm not mistaken, celebrated well beyond Kentucky. Coming across him somewhere recently, I jotted down this short poem of his:

> Why all the embarrassment
> about being happy?
> Sometimes I'm as happy
> as a sleeping dog,
> and for the same reasons,
> and for others.

What might a sleeping dog's reasons be, by the way? You think you know, but do you? Berry has an inkling it's because they have no forethought of grief—they know grief, yes, but do not contemplate its arrival. Nor, it would seem, does the poet. I would also like to know what 'other' reasons Wendell Berry might have for being happy. High dopamine levels, some will suggest, might play a part, especially these days when neuropsychological explanations for things are simply common wisdom. In sophisticated circles you argue with neuroscience at your peril, people look at you askance, as if you'd embraced Deepak Chopra or someone even dottier. Neurotransmitters explain a lot, I'm sure, yet surely there are other, more nuanced reasons for happiness as well.

One good reason I have for feeling happy towards the end of a long life is the vivid sense I have of flowering at last. Hope, which is the mainstay of so many theories of happiness, is more or less beyond my grasp at this point, but I'm aware of a burgeoning at work deep inside me, an opening up, a many-hued efflorescence that is less 'outer', so to speak, than 'inner'. (The two are intertwined, I know, yet not the same.) I attribute this flowering in large part to having finally 'run out of bullshit', as the Peter Finch character put it in the movie *Network*, although in my case in a good way. When Howard Beale, the news anchorman played by Finch, ran out of bullshit ('the God bullshit', for instance, the noble hero bullshit, the married-with-kids bullshit, and all the other reasons people give for putting up with the pointless pain of staying alive), he was left feeling so empty he decided to shoot his brains out in the middle of the television news. Mad as hell, he famously refused to take it any more.

While I understand his anger—the world is indeed a 'demented slaughterhouse', amongst other things, and our attempts to find a point in surviving it futile—I confess that I've experienced the drying up of bullshit more as a liberation than a hollowing out, as Howard Beale did. And that is because, less encumbered now by the bossy ideologies that once propped me up, my inner life has noticeably unfurled in recent years, quite luxuriantly in spots—in fact, I'd even say that my inner life has 'blossomed' if that didn't sound so twee. Without all those layers of bullshit clogging it, I'm freer to agree or disagree these days with supposedly self-evident truths, to care or not care as I wish about things (whether of cosmic significance or of no account at all)—and even to say so, cutting through the humbug. I've been waiting a whole lifetime for this kind of *ease*.

How can anyone contemplate old age and its discontents without an inner life, I wonder, wandering amongst the clouds of pink azaleas and beds of yellow pansies. As the idea of a soul falls apart, what else is there to give our sense of self some cohesion? Towards the end, the physical self also falls apart as the body tires of pretending to be a 'system' and turns into a killing field, swarming with warring factions of microbes. What might hold you together more reliably than a soul in the traditional sense or mind-body therapies, it seems to me, especially in your later years, is a sturdy mental core. In a word, an intricately configured life of the mind.

Going cold turkey on a self is admittedly difficult. Susan Sontag went even further, famously declaring that death was *unbearable* unless you could 'get beyond the "I"', which, naturally enough, she failed to do. Barbara Ehrenreich, another fearless thinker, also links the fear of death to the illusion of selfhood, wondering in *Natural Causes*, her recent book on ageing, if in the future, psychedelic drugs might be the key to dissolving all fear of death as we get older by destroying the illusion of a unitary self. Is there no better option than this? Half the middle-aged population lying about high on acid? In reality I think the *actually* old—at least those with normal egos—are remarkably sanguine about death, I don't think many of us find death 'unbearable' at all. It's the process of dying we're fearful of.

Then it strikes me: I keep coming back to the idea of an inner life, but I am actually confused about what an inner life is. Wending my way along the dank pathways between the banks of azaleas, dodging the scratchy fern fronds (so full of life, this hidden garden, even in winter, so nose-pinchingly *fecund* somehow), I start searching for words to describe more realistically what it is I mean by the term. It's so *slow* out here in the garden, time's dawdling, I can think. Beyond the walls of the mossy garden I'm in I can hear the world roaring.

It's best to steer well clear of anything with even the whiff of a soul about it nowadays—that goes without saying. Once upon a time we would trade our very bodies for a soul (repress our bodies, scourge our bodies), whereas what souls make me picture now is poached eggs—as they do the British comedian, Steve Coogan, I note: squishy and easily spilt. The educated classes won't stand for this sort of mumbo-jumbo. While they like to celebrate 'difference', as they call it, some things are acceptably different (hijabs, for instance) while other things, such as souls (not unrelated to the wearing of hijabs, as it happens), are not. Ernest Becker phrases it a little more politely: 'most modern Westerners,' he writes, 'will have trouble believing' in souls and so on any more—in essences of any kind, in fact. Yet it is precisely this drift into hypermodernity I would like to resist; as the body falls apart, I'm holding fast to something still unbroken. How can I do this without sounding half-witted? I stop to study a pansy that has caught my eye—a tiny burst of yellow and magenta amidst the mossiness in this part of the garden—and wonder if music might hold the key.

Along with 'soul', I'm avoiding 'spiritual'. It's a popular word for the uplifting feelings and emotions you experience when contemplating things much vaster than yourself, things that pass all understanding, such as the rumoured oneness of everything or sites sacred to indigenous peoples or at a pinch to the Japanese. Half the atheists I know claim to feel 'spiritual' when they're far from human habitation contemplating the night sky. If there's one thing that rattles atheists it's feeling they might be missing out on something that wishy-washy believers have access to. Meditation, too, makes some of its practitioners feel 'spiritual'. Is it the god pose? Unsurprisingly, Ernest Becker lists trying to be godlike as one of the most common death-avoidance techniques across the globe. Actually, anything Himalayan risks being called 'spiritual'. Foreigners regularly feel 'spiritual' in India in general. Do they mean 'beyond time'? I suspect 'spiritual' might often be an attempt to describe the feeling of timelessness. Surely we can do better than 'spiritual'. 'Mental life', though, sounds a touch clinical for my purposes and 'intellectual life' too biased towards reason and ideas. 'A life of the mind' captures well what I think is so important if we are to age well. I suppose I mean by a 'life of the mind' a coherent self-understanding deeply rooted in ways of being and thinking going back forever. And I mean *forever*, like an infinite hall of mirrors of self-reflection, like a complex piece of music, too, shaped by centuries beyond number.

Everyone loves music—from archbishops to atheists, from small children to professors of psychiatry at the Harvard Medical School, everyone everywhere stops for music. In a few corners of Afghanistan, where religion feels its hegemony threatened by music, it's still forbidden—which rather proves the point I'm trying to make, surely—but nearly everywhere else loving music is an essential part of being human. Music, of course, actually configures time, it does not, as some new-age practices claim to do, touch time with a magic wand and make it disappear.

An abundant, intricately patterned life of the mind would be a tall order at St Ursula's. Failing health and decaying minds are everywhere you look here. Illness, decrepitude and dementia. The sounds of madness rustle and reverberate up and down the corridors, the smells of sickness hang in the air. Even the sane seem slightly gaga, the healthy hunched and tilted. It shakes me every time I see it. We know about it, we've known all our lives, yet when you come face to face with it, it shocks you, it claws at your heart. It's exactly what shook Siddhartha Gautama to his core, after all, when he first ventured beyond his palace gardens: the sight of an old man. The next time he left his palace, he saw a diseased man, then a rotting corpse and finally an ascetic. How to live amidst such endless suffering? How to find a pathway through it?

All I can do in this regard, since I am as much a foreigner in these matters as I am in Java, is try to navigate my way between sentiment on the one hand and neurology on the other, my mind homing in on something more Horatian: living through to a fine old age. That's my middle way. Needless to say, it's hardly Siddhartha Buddha's middle way, and my aim is never nirvana but simply *une belle vieillesse*, as the French call it with rather more panache than English-speakers can muster. 'Good' is too wishy-washy for the French, too easily confused with 'virtuous'—they rightly aim for beauty. Virtuosity has little to do with virtue.

With the ornate tracery of high notes now fading in my head, I make my way back inside into the fug of B Wing. What does it smell of? Something slightly sour. Sickly sour. Just faintly clammy. Josie's sitting in the sunroom in her nightie and dressing-gown, her face bright and blank. Or is her name Janice? She never speaks, she only whistles, so I can't ask her to tell me. This morning she's whistling something I could swear is from *Oklahoma!* It's quite a warm, pretty room, and if you crane your neck you can glimpse the river through the greenery. The corridor leading to Rita's room is deserted, though. I try not to look into the rooms with the doors left open—not that I'd see anything too distressing, just a bed, a chair and an old woman, I'd see lives that have shrunk now to little more than a bed and a chair by the window, with perhaps a singalong at Christmas.

To my surprise, Rita is now sitting up; she's propped up with cushions in the chair by the window. Not exactly bright-eyed and bushy-tailed, but still—it's like a resurrection. There's only one chair, so Peter is perched on the edge of the bed. There's a slightly crooked smile on her thin, bruised face.

'Hullo, darling!' I think, but would never say aloud. How could I say 'darling'? And so I say: 'You're up!' and go over and kiss her on her cheekbone.

'Haven't they got any?' she asks.

'Not yet, no,' I say. Nowadays we just play along with this sort of thing. What can it possibly matter? 'Would you like the television on?'

'Have you got a cold, Olive?'

'No, Rita, I'm fine,' I say and give her gaunt cheek another peck.

'Isn't it quiet!' No, it's not, really, this afternoon, what with her neighbour crying out 'Somebody help me!' ceaselessly and the clang of the trolley, but Rita's deaf.

'Would you like the television on?'

'It's so quiet.'

'Yes,' we murmur, 'it is.'

'Can I go home now?'

There's a knock on the door and Eddy sweeps in, jaunty in white, with Rita's tray. 'Hullo, Rita, sweetheart! Are we ready for lunch?'

What a farce. It smells mouth-wateringly good—the

roast chicken in gravy, the cake in custard, the coffee, the warm bread roll—as hospital and airline food always does, whatever the picky might say to the contrary, but Rita won't touch any of it. 'That looks good, Mum!' Peter says cheerily.

'Doesn't it just!' says Eddy, agleam with unguents.

But Rita won't eat any of it—that's the point. She'll fiddle for a while with a Tim-Tam from the bedside table, dropping crumbs and chocolate flakes all over everything, and then ask us when we're going to leave. But first she'll flirt with Eddy. She's ninety-five, skeletal, gaga, and never liked men anyway, yet first she'll flirt with Eddy. And why not?

'Will *you* take me home?' she asks him as he brings the back of her chair forward. Not a bad line at any age.

'Only if you eat this all up, sweetheart,' he says.

Rita chokes briefly and then smiles demurely. 'I want to go home,' she says.

Rita, darling, you are home. This, Rita, is it. This room, this chair, this bed and the cross above it are *it*.

I wonder, as I often do, if Rita ever had a real inner life. She is kind, if not quite to a fault, and sometimes sharp, but, knowing her as I have for over thirty years,

I have seen few signs of a patterned inner life. She used to knit, watch the cricket and the football on TV, now and again bought clothes, more for something to do than from any need of new blouses or shoes, cooked biscuits until quite recently, and every year sent Christmas cards to members of her family she otherwise never spoke to. She didn't gossip, didn't read, never went to the cinema or listened to music—had no obvious interest in anything at all, really, except us. Once a week she liked to play solo with a few other women from the Village, until one by one, like Olive, they went deaf or blind or simply died, as people do. Over time I've met quite a few women of her generation and background with little inner life. It's not a lack of intelligence, it's … what?

'It's time for me to go,' she says, as she does every day. It is, of course, not quite as simple as that.

Sorry for Your Loss

Was that the noonday call to prayer starting to swell across the fields? The cries rising from scores of minarets came swarming across the plain towards where I sat, a rising wave of high-pitched wailing. I floated up on the surge ... *Allahu akbar, 'ashadu 'an la 'ilaha 'illa-llah* ... And then came the jolting blast from the mosque beside the hotel: *'Allahu Akbar, 'Ashadu 'An La 'Ilaha 'Illa-Llah* ... And then from the mosque just beyond the hotel: *'Allahu Akbar, 'Ashadu* ... The cries hit me like flashes of lightning. And they were taken up by the muezzin in the next village, and the next and the next and the next. When the last call faded and the stillness returned, I thought to myself that amongst all those mosques and prayer-halls people no doubt had many ways of speaking forthrightly about death.

In our sort of society, unchurched as it largely is, if not yet completely unbelieving, it's sometimes claimed that the only weapon left in our arsenal for 'destroying the last enemy' is avoiding the subject. In more traditional societies, however, people have long-established approaches to talking about death, dealing with loss and grief in ways that make death seem an everyday part of life, almost fun: they offer up prayers, they have colourful mourning ceremonies, they have acceptable religious clichés to exchange about paradise or reincarnation or some other afterlife. We have nothing, except the fatuous 'Sorry for your loss', which makes it sound as if you caused it. Yet even a century or more ago the French writer André Gide, who was rarely at a loss for words, was tongue-tied in a similar situation. When the young wife of a servant he was particularly fond of suddenly died, Gide, a non-believer, went over to his house with his sister-in-law, Jeanne Drouin, to offer his sincerely felt condolences. He shook the grieving man's hand without saying a word, 'too deeply moved to be able to speak'. His sister-in-law, however, who was a Christian, began speaking to Marius from her heart. She found a wealth of things to say to him—consoling things, full of pity but also hope, all said in exactly the right tone of voice. Your beloved young wife is now waiting for you in heaven, she said, where she has taken her place among the angels, she's thinking about you constantly, watching over you, loving and protecting you, all the while singing beautiful hymns. And Gide was full of wonder as he listened that religious belief could provoke 'such a sincere outpouring of feeling', whereas all his friendship for Marius left him with nothing to say at all.

In contemporary times, death just embarrasses us, it seems, or makes us squeamish. I'm not sure even traditional societies always offer mourners much to say of substance—in Torajaland, for example, north of here just below the equator in Sulawesi, I discovered that even the Toraja, who seem to spend half their waking lives at rituals for the dead, are left with little to say to the bereaved except 'I'm so sorry'. At any hour of the day or night, it seemed to me, there are thousands of Toraja in black, crammed onto the back of trucks, careering cheerily across the lush landscape, up and down the mountains, in and out of the forests, on their way to yet another funeral. At least they still have an abundance of noisy ceremonial ways of farewelling the dead.

These days, further from the equator, not only our doctors but even our clergymen will often avoid looking death in the eye for fear of offending or even nauseating us. Now, if you're really finding it hard to cope, you'd do best to call Lifeline or Beyond Blue and discuss it with someone you can't see. Still, when grandpa finally 'passes on' (or simply 'passes', as everyone has mysteriously taken to saying recently, as if leaving 'on' out lets you off the awkward hook of having to imagine where to) you have to do something. Which bit of grandpa is it that passes, one wonders. Are there actually two grandpas: the one you burn and the one that floats off to rest somewhere in eternal peace? Is one of those an illusion? Which one? You can't give him a send-off by sacrificing bullocks, as the Toraja do, or burn him with a strangled slave girl on a ship like a Volga Viking, but you have to come up with *something* to do. *Faute de mieux*, a few members of grandpa's family and a clutch of his mates might get together to 'celebrate his life'. After a burst of '*I did it my way*' (how he loved that song!), a few hilarious stories will be recounted about the larks he used to get up to at the bowling club Christmas party every year. Talk about a larrikin! Small advertisements will appear under Death Notices in the local newspaper, assuring anyone who peruses it that he is sorely missed. If he was once a politician, someone will say 'Vale'. (The Latin commits you to nothing, yet is manly.) That's about it. Bereft of rituals and shared beliefs, that's as much as we can usually manage. It's as if we were repaying a small, unspecified debt, but since it's a *small* one, there's no need to say anything too genuinely heartfelt—no emotional cats need be let unexpectedly out of any bags. Or is the deceased repaying a small debt to us? Quite a few mourners, one has the impression, are there because they really do want to be in at the end, so to speak. They're owed a final performance.

Even in the presence of the body of someone we've greatly loved, we Westerners shrink from looking. For centuries in Europe even the casket was concealed. All the same, whether we can see it or not, we do like to know there's a body there. We like to have a body to formally dispose of, it's true, even if nobody needs to see it.

Occasionally, someone will even appear on television claiming in all seriousness to have at last found closure, now that the bones of a great-grandfather they never knew have been identified in some corner of Belgium and ceremoniously, by unknown hands, out of sight, laid to rest. Senseless butchery has been redeemed, it would appear. The more overtly meaningless the deaths, as when a tsunami strikes or a volcanic eruption wipes out whole towns—children, grandmothers, dogs, parrots, the lot—the more fervent the rites become. After any event of mass extinction, a rationalist will be tempted to imagine that it must be evident by now to anyone but the seriously unhinged that nobody is in charge, no being or presence of any kind, supreme, tutelary, numinous, omnipotent or anything else—there or not there, nobody knows, but clearly not in charge. Yet at precisely such times ceremonial religion goes into overdrive. Priests rush to the scene in their long robes, ringing bells and beseeching a hidden almighty spirit to show loving-kindness, before the emergency service vehicles can even drive off with the dying and the dead (bagged). Humans need a framework of meaning to slot the deaths into, however irrational its provenance might be. The less meaning we can come up with, in other words, for what is actually the case, the more extravagant the ceremonies. But we don't want to look at bodies.

If the encyclopaedically knowledgeable historian of death and dying in Europe, Philippe Ariès, is to be believed, we've been keen to conceal dead bodies in Western Europe in whatever way we can since the 1200s. A dead body is now regarded as 'improper', as he puts it, even 'a nauseating spectacle' we must be shielded from. In earlier times we hugged and fondled the corpse, kissed it on the mouth, combed its hair and wailed over it, just as King Arthur and his knights did (according to the legend) whenever someone close to them was killed, but since the Catholic Church took over the death business, Ariès contends, the corpse has assumed a sort of 'magical' power and so can no longer be simply sewn up in a deer-skin bag or wrapped in a shroud and planted somewhere. Until the uncertainty over precisely what is immortal, where it lives immortally, and its connection with the observable universe can be sorted out, Western Christians have mostly thought it best to keep the corpse wrapped and out of sight from the moment it stops breathing. The sheet is pulled up and that's the end of that.

Christians seem confused about what exactly is supposed to be immortal in a way most heathens (or

Buddhists or Hindus) are not. The story of Jesus' bodily reappearance after his execution has left Christians with a problem no Muslim—anybody else at all—has. Is the body itself in some baffling way immortal, Christians must ask themselves, able to be revitalised, reinhabited on Jesus' return by the soul that once left it? Can the grandpa we knew so well, the grey-haired former accountant cremated at Northern Suburbs Crematorium, be reunited with a second, phantom grandpa, of unknown substance or hair colour, going about his business in another dimension, and rise again? Or is immortality reserved for the disembodied? What is the connection between the body and the afterlife, if any?

During the Late Middle Ages, certain corpses, and in particular saintly corpses, not waiting for Jesus' return, were on occasion confusingly infused with life-signs—they winked, failed to decompose, grew hair and sometimes made a little light conversation, usually with each other. I have myself marvelled at St Francis Xavier's miraculously incorrupt cadaver, for instance (minus an arm that was touring Canada at the time of my visit), encased in a glass box inside a silver casket in the Basilica of Bom Jesus in Goa. Although not averse to burning any number of Hindus to death for failing to convert to Catholicism, right there in the plaza next to the Basilica, the Spaniard is looking astonishingly alive, if not exactly well, himself. (Or was it next to the Cathedral he had them burnt? I saw so many unutterably beautiful Catholic churches in Goa that it is hard to remember now which was which.) In other words, his corpse and his essential being are still in touch with each other in a recognisably Christian way. In Sicily, where the Middle Ages arguably lasted longer than in most of Europe, the stocks of mummies in the Capuchin Catacombs of Palermo were replenished right up until the 1920s and can be viewed 365 days a year, including Christmas, in all their spell-bindingly macabre variety: friars, children, women, sitting slumped against each other, lying, even standing, open-mouthed, eyes closed, eyes wide open. According to the Sicilian osteologist and bioarcheologist Dario Piombino-Mascali, an expert on the catacombs, Sicilians used mummification 'to make sure there was a constant relationship between life and death'. (Which I would understand to mean 'constant *signs* of a relationship'.) On certain feast days the family of the corpse could even hold hands with it, inviting it to join them in prayer—for a fee, naturally, payable to the Capuchins.

Muslims, while they have relics, don't go in for this sort of thing at all. The body rots, the soul survives. The mummified son of the King of Tunis, for instance, can be viewed in the Capuchin Catacombs, but he had to convert to Catholicism first.

Just across the water from Java in Torajaland, with its ancient animist traditions, there is again no confusion at all about what is mortal and what is immortal. The old woman's body I sat beside in her bedroom in a house in Pangala would be considered alive—'gravely ill', to be precise—until it was ceremonially entombed in a cavity in a nearby rock-face in a few months' time or even the following year, depending on how long it took to bring all her relatives back to Pangala for the funeral from Jakarta, Toronto, Melbourne and wherever else they'd ended up, as well as to scrape together the enormous amount of money the whole extravaganza would cost. Apart from anything else, many bullocks and pigs would have to be slaughtered—her noble soul needed the bovine souls to ride to paradise on—and that would be expensive. Until this could all be arranged, her soul would be hovering, waiting, in a sort of limbo (*puya*) from where, once all the ceremonies had been correctly performed, on the back of a phantom buffalo, her spirit would journey on to the centre of the universe (*batara maya* in Torajan). There was nothing magical about the body, nothing to be dreaded, not the slightest hint of the numinous. Beside me was a body, in that house I chanced upon, embalmed with herbs, sweet-smelling, with the hair nicely brushed, lying dead in bed. Hovering close by was the *bombo*, the ghostly self. There was no confusion about what was what. Meanwhile, the family was going noisily about its business around us, from time to time offering us buns, dried banana slices and cups of tea.

In some villages, once a year, in August, the mummified bodies are taken out of their cavities in the cliff-faces, washed, dressed afresh—given an 'airing' (*angin-anginan*), as they put it—and then sealed up again in their cavity, sometimes with an effigy at the entrance. In other words, the send-off is never-ending. I don't suppose we present-day Westerners belong anywhere as strongly as the Toraja do to their villages, so farewelling the dead once is enough for us.

In the highlands of Madagascar there are also regular exhumations of the dead, with wild partying accompanying the reburial in fresh winding cloths. I wonder if this ritualised veneration of the corpse was brought to Madagascar by the first migrants from the Malay archipelago 1200 years ago—perhaps it's originally a Malay custom. There's a bit of regular 'bone-washing' still going on in a Mayan village in Mexico as well—there the bones are cleaned once a year and placed in a fresh shroud for reinterment with offerings of flowers and lit candles—but for the most part, after the first funeral, Mexicans make do with spirits.

In the wake of the Enlightenment in Europe, fewer people looked to the notion of a second, ghostly self for consolation. The body was increasingly understood as a kind of mechanical contraption that would one day seize up and stop working, while the soul was generally left to its own devices. A ghost or two might appear at night if the death had been shockingly premature, but nothing verifiable. Death was to be regretted, but was no longer *terrifying*. Nor is it now. Frightening, alarming, distressing, but not unspeakably *terrifying*.

Saying goodbye is painful, however, for those

leaving as well as those staying behind, piercingly painful. Saying goodbye is harrowing, it cuts you to the quick. And so we seek, each people in its own way, to make it part of life. In some places, as I've mentioned, where they are less squeamish about bodies than we are, they have, I know, come up with unusual parting ceremonies, face-to-dead-face, full-body parting ceremonies that make our sedate gatherings at the graveside or at the bowling club seem shallow and emotionally stunting. In Japan, for instance, family and friends might gather in a room in the house to watch a loved one carefully washed down and ceremonially swathed in colourful silks, the face (shaved right there in front of them, if it's a man) enlivened with make-up, the lips painted as everyone silently looks on, the hair combed, the body then placed in a casket with a special window in the lid allowing everyone present to keep their eyes on the face until at the very last moment the window is gently closed. It is a slow farewell. It is a formal departure. There is weeping, but no wailing. There is bowing, but no performance. Or at least that is how it all played out in *Departures*, the movie I saw about saying goodbye in modern Japan. I hope it's true. Of course, in Japan the railways employ people to wave goodbye to trains. That sort of ritual simply wouldn't work where I live any more than the feasting and incantations of the Toraja would. Before the death of the body we are speechless. We have not managed to make saying goodbye part of life at all.

The ritualised devotion to human remains seems at least in part to be a long-drawn-out farewell, as it was in the days of King Arthur and Charlemagne in Europe. Without a body to perform some kind of rites over, we still feel we can't say goodbye properly, in a soul-satisfying way. ('Inwardly satisfying' doesn't quite capture the feeling.) There's no need to sacrifice buffaloes since we don't believe our souls will have need of theirs in the afterlife, and we expect no supernatural signs of life in the corpse, even if it's a nun's or saint's, and according to scholars such as Ariès and Boase we've had little *coherent* belief in an afterlife since about 1400, but all the same we do like to take our leave with a bit of music and dressing-up—and at least the suggestion of a body. When capitalism and religiosity converged (almost riotously on high occasions), the Victorians turned mourning into an extravaganza of feathers, silk and velvet, as Dickens noted, and cemeteries from mere fields of repose as they had once been into magnificent cities of the dead. For the moneyed classes the brouhaha and pageantry worked well. Nowadays, without religion as our superego, we're left with just the capitalism part. It's not very emotionally satisfying. Believing in nothing, when all is said and done, not even an essential self, we still have a lingering need for a body to say goodbye to.

All the same, now that people are less understood as bodies than as tweets, perhaps even the need for an actual body to give a send-off to will eventually fade. We'll just tweet R.I.P. or some other hocus-pocus into cyberspace, and carry on chatting.

※

From another point of view, I thought, eyeing a brood of ducklings darting across the path in front of me, headed for the paddy opposite—well, for the oven eventually, of course, but for the time being just for the paddy on the other side—our society never shuts up about death and dying. Death at a distance is the epitome of good entertainment. Even children's video games are about annihilation. Sometimes it seems as if death is just about the only show in town: as I walk towards the wall of new movies at my local suburban video store (being old enough to think this a completely normal thing to do), a whole slew of DVD cases comes into focus, depicting death by shooting, bombing, knifing, mutilation, strangling and driving over cliffs. Killing is what at least half of the new movies feature. Even the madcap comedies are about terminal illness and fatal car-crashes. On television we have programs about pathological killers, death squads and homicidal vicars lurking in the English countryside, we have youth suicide, agonising death in the emergency ward and police dramas about catching killers—and that's before we get to the catalogue of deaths on the late news: apart from the untimely deaths at home, there will be thousands dead in distant earthquakes and mudslides, mass drownings at sea, the daily brutal slaughter in Indonesian abattoirs, in conflicts in Afghanistan and Iraq, and from police violence in East Africa or the United States. Rita used to say that in those countries people are at least used to it. I'm getting pretty used to it myself. By bedtime I've seen dozens of people die on camera and the aftermath of scores of other deaths. Every night. My morning newspaper nowadays reports virtually nothing apart from murder, disease and sexual abuse: it might take the odd pot-shot at a politician, devote one or two pieces to solar power or immigration, but basically it's death and sex.

No, we are not at all shy about discussing death *as such*. In fact, we gorge ourselves daily on fictional deaths and the deaths of others. Talking, and even thinking, about our own extinction is less common, however. It can scarcely be borne. Once it dawned on the philosopher Montaigne that the game would one day be up not only for humanity at large (something he could bear—well, the Wars of Religion raged for most of his adult life, so he had to have some way of coping with boundless bloodshed), but also for Michel Yquem de Montaigne himself, member of the landed gentry, rich on salt herring and wine, owner of vast estates near Bordeaux. Once he'd taken this fact about his own life in, he began 'philosophising' day in and day out to fortify himself against the crucial final scene of the last act. What is philosophising, after all, as he himself pointed out, harking back to Cicero, but a preparation for death—'learning how to die'? Fantasies about what happens after death are the province of religion, while thinking about how to live happily, given an ending, is the philosopher's business. Few of us have the tools to follow Montaigne's example.

Instead of 'philosophising', most of us keep the profounder questions about life and death at bay by giving our minds over to trivia. Margaret Drabble, whose eccentric photographic portrait by Mayotte Magnus hangs in the National Portrait Gallery in London, unmissably right by the escalator, writes illuminatingly about this ploy in *The Dark Flood Rises*, a whole novel about old age and its discontents, the canvas so broad and entertainingly detailed you might even wonder from time to time if there can be much point in being young. Teresa, one of her main characters, a Catholic still uncommitted to the idea of an afterlife, is fascinated to discover while resting one day with a book on the Etruscans in her comfortable apartment in an aged-care facility that both pain and trivia can be a welcome distraction from the ultimately serious business of dying. Pain alters perceptions of time, and makes one wish to be elsewhere, whereas trivia comfortably and companionably block the forefront of the mind, occupying the space that might otherwise be devoted to prayer or thought or meditation or despair.

Trivia, for Teresa, might mean a book on your lap, a radio quiz, a text message or two, a mug of soup, or a nice, warm blanket over her knees. Cars, golf and keeping fit are also classed by Teresa as 'trivia', although male trivia, rather than the kind that cushion her own thoughts. Trivia have no roots, at least in *your* life. Like jigsaw puzzles, sports results and what other people's children are up to, they have no consequences beyond the moment—for *us*. (And so the weather used to be trivial as a conversational gambit, but no longer is.) Not just Christmas and the British royal family, but these days whole art galleries, top to bottom, college courses, newspapers, indeed entire media networks, are monuments to trivia. From Greenland to Tasmania, entire lives, generation after generation, are submerged in oceans of gossamer-thin trivia. An afternoon or two of pure trivia now and then can indeed be refreshing, obviously, as can gossiping or playing bridge or badminton in the park—what could be more amusing and life-affirming that watching Nigella Lawson pointlessly tossing a Moroccan salad?—but a lifetime of triteness is surely a tragedy. At a certain point in anyone's life, it goes without saying, few things will have any consequence beyond the moment—apart from the terms of one's will. All the same, it's worth resisting this thinning out of memory in whatever way we can. Our cores won't stay strong on pap.

Your death is difficult for me to talk about with you, especially face to face. If you're a friend of mine, or even a chance acquaintance, somebody I've just met on a tram, say, I'd feel as squeamish talking to you about your death as my own. It wouldn't be quite taboo, but almost. The millions dying of air pollution every year in India and China are easy enough to discuss, but your mortality is almost impossible to touch upon, except in terms of your will or your preferred funeral arrangements. Your grief is particularly embarrassing. We murmur some cliché or other awkwardly—'He's in a better place', 'Do let me know if there's anything I can do'—as if discountenanced by your misery. We're unnerved as well these days by the idea of nothingness, I suppose—contemplating nothingness makes everyone feel uncomfortable. Less terrified than once was the case perhaps, but unsettled. The room goes quiet if you point out that, *as far as anybody knows*, Kevin or Irene no longer exists, is now as non-existent as Cinderella. Some version of Kevin or Irene may indeed now be at one with a timeless Being in some other dimension. All the same, as far as anybody knows or has *reason* to believe, including the Archbishop of Canterbury and the Regius Professor of Divinity at Christ Church, Oxford, Kevin and Irene are nought. There is no incontrovertible proof that anything apart from decaying body parts survives the shutting down of the body. None. There is no purely rational reason to believe that anything we knew as Kevin or Irene has gone to 'a better place' any more than a dead geranium has. Faith and hope require no rational reasons for flourishing, but belief does.

Is there no comfort to be had anywhere in the face of death? Is the battle against 'the last enemy' futile?

The battle to defeat death bodily certainly looks doomed. The well-tended body shows every sign of falling apart and rotting at more or less the same age the well-tended body has always fallen apart and rotted at, even in Ancient Greece: at the age I am now—three score years and ten plus a bit. Seventh-Day Adventists rarely outlive Sophocles although they apparently live much longer than anyone else does. A lifetime's wholesomeness will strike some of us as a high price to pay for just ten extra years.

Notions of a soul offer little consolation, either, in the face of mortality in the early twenty-first century. When it comes to traditional souls (bodiless crystallisations of the personality, sometimes with arms and legs, sometimes not), the future seems bleak. Millions still pin their hopes on a soul, reconfiguring it in some circles as an electromagnetic force field, but it all sounds pretty pie in the sky to me. The New Jerusalem that John of Patmos saw in a vision and wrote about in the Book of Revelation promises a vast city of the saved in which there will be 'no more death', and God will wipe away all tears, and there will be 'neither sorrow, nor crying, neither shall there be any more pain ...' How many people take this promise seriously any more? Was John's vision of a 'spiritual' city full of souls or just a city, like Warsaw, say, only bigger, and full of immortal physical bodies? As usual, Christians seem divided. Their imaginations seem to have failed them. If we're reluctant to give up entirely on an eternal soul, we may resort to 'faith' in it, just to keep our hand in. Faith is what you have when you actually have no idea what's going on, it's hope that you admit in advance is groundless.

Or you might settle for something that is neither a body nor a soul: an inner life. Fashion it as you will. Since those moments in the garden at St Ursula's, I like to think of an inner life as if it were a cherished piece of music: an intricate composition, deeply felt (not simply understood), springing from a shared cultural bedrock, although shaped by our own individual memories over a lifetime. It is the lifeblood of our imagination. This composition doesn't have to be Beethoven's Ninth. The overarching sense of meaning that such an inner life furnishes us with can serve as a bulwark against the constant splintering of meaning, the relentless breaking-up of memory into scattered shards, that the world of digitalised chatter and aimless velocity exacerbates. It eases our anxiety about our ageing bodies, about the slow collapse of our outer selves, trapped by the clock, by entropy; and it gives us heart in the face of the loneliness that comes with the emptying out of the world we were once at home in, the culling (not always gentle) of our intimate friends. At the Grange, you notice that room after room after room, as you walk up the corridor to Rita's, is empty but for the gaunt figure in the bed, dozing or staring forlornly at the ceiling. It is a wasteland of solitariness. A vibrant life of the mind, if it grows out of something much wider and richer than just you, might people the inner spaces, if I might put it like that, in a way that makes the solitude a little more bearable. Even the fear of death and dying, it seems to me, if we do indeed fear it, might seem less tyrannical, less terrifying, if our self-understanding were multilayered and strong. ('There is no loneliness,' wrote the Persian Sufi Hafiz in one of his ecstatic poems, 'to the clear-eyed mystic / In this luminous, brimming / Playful world.' But those lines were written 700 years ago in Shiraz, or possibly Isfahan, far from St Ursula's.)

Meanwhile, it's lunchtime. It's time to turn back to the hotel for a spot of sustenance. Something crisp and spicy would be nice ... a prawn spring roll? *Lumpia udang* with a tiny dish of soy sauce. A glass of guava juice. I stood stock-still for a moment there at the edge of the village, just looking and listening and smelling the smoky earthiness of everything and thinking about death and prawn spring rolls and guava juice. I felt at that instant almost surreally foreign and alone. Abruptly, as I stood there motionless in the silence, the elaborate systems of signs and emblems I had grown up amongst and loved, the clusterings of people I thought of as like-minded and liked to mingle with, were little more than wisps of cloud in an infinite sky. Sultry climes often have this effect on me. So for some mysterious reason does anything even faintly Hindu. I never felt at all like that while living in Finland.

Oddly enough, I thought to myself, breathing in the smell of rotting papayas and muddy drains, without death there is no meaning. Without time nothing is of any consequence. Time allows hope. Time makes us feel intensely alive. It's just that it runs out. Well, there you go. Dizzy with the stench of putrifying fruit, at that precise moment I didn't much care.

Fretting about Nothing

Sarah certainly wasn't 'looking like shit' next morning, as she claimed she generally did: she was slightly crumpled if you looked closely, but quite jaunty. *Soignée* as always, in pale turquoise. Since we were on our way to Borobudur, a spectacular monument to nothingness, it seemed the perfect moment, once we'd left the messy sprawl of Yogyakarta behind, to bring up the subject of nothingness. Was nothingness one of the things Sarah thought those striving to stay young were hoping to hold at bay? Did people these days really fear their own eventual extinction? The endless indignities and maladies of ageing perhaps, the pain, the loneliness and boredom, but utter annihilation? 'Death' was not particular enough.

'I'm not sure many of us even try to picture becoming

nothing, to be honest, let alone fear it,' she said. 'Do you find it scary? Strictly speaking, not even Borobudur is a monument to nothingness, I gather.' She gazed thoughtfully out of the window at the bustling somethingness we were surrounded by, stuck behind a truck, then she coughed in that very particular way she has of coughing. It makes me think of chalk dust, but then we did first meet all those decades ago in a classroom. She'd been doing her homework. She really was in excellent spirits this morning. Java does that to you, I find, early in the day, wherever you are. She squinted at her *Lonely Planet* guide. 'When they say "nothingness",' she went on, 'I think they actually mean "emptiness", which is not quite the same thing. The idea of a void.'

'I certainly find the idea of a *void* terrifying,' I said, 'but nothingness not so much.' I was traumatised in 1980 by the opening scenes of *Superman II*, in which Zod, his evil consort Ursa and a hulking mute called Non are flattened into thin plates and hurled into 'the phantom zone' to spin in infinite emptiness forever, 'an eternal living death'. I've never quite got over it. Anyway, it's on YouTube.

'We can ask someone about it when we get there.'

She stared out of the window. 'By the way, what the hell is *bakso*? Do you know? *Bakso* this, *bakso* that.'

On every side as far as the eye could see, restaurants, simple teahouses, even street vendors with their steaming food carts, were selling *bakso*. *Bakso* soup, *bakso* with noodles, fried *bakso*, fish and beef and chicken *bakso*, egg *bakso* and mushroom *bakso*. There was no respite from the signs for *bakso*. The locals were clearly crazy about meatballs. The roadside where we were caught in the traffic jam was a grubby profusion of shirt shops, mobile-phone shops, antique furniture shops, television shops, even pet-care shops, that seemed to go on forever, sprouting here beyond the city limits like mushrooms after rain. Now and again, as we inched forwards, behind the endless *scabbiness* we could glimpse blue-green hills. When would we turn off the road into the green? The green began just a stone's throw away, the quiet and the green, right behind the places selling gravestones, plaster geese, ganeshas and galvanised iron there were stands of palm-trees.

'Calling it "emptiness" is all very well,' I said, after rather too long a pause, but alert as ever for humbug, 'but empty of what?'

'We'll have to ask. The self, I think. But there's light, I read somewhere, the emptiness is light-filled.'

'Well, that really does scare the shit out of me. It sounds exactly like an eternal St Ursula's Grange—the place where Rita is incarcerated: empty and light-filled, all ego crushed. "Empty" makes it sound as if there's nothing *there*, but there's still a *there*, if you see what I mean. What I'm wondering is if people are afraid of being totally extinguished. Do you remember when I … you know … *died*, not to put too fine a point on it, and they had to paddle me back to life?'

'Actually died? *No*. Really?'

'Yes, it's in the cardiology report.'

'Goodness. How could I have forgotten?'

Indeed. 'I think you'd just had your stroke at the time,' I said, 'so there was a lot going on. Anyway, everyone, even the medical students who were always hanging around the foot of the bed asking questions, asked me if there'd been anything *there*.'

'Well, had there?'

'Where? The point is that *there is no "there"*, Sarah. That's what I mean by nothingness. When the penny drops, does this frighten anyone?'

'Oh, I see,' she said, offering me a mint. 'No, I don't think that's what the Buddhists mean by emptiness, is it? You know, you're reminding me of a conversation I once had about this very thing with an intense young man in Cairo.'

'I wish I'd been there.'

'He was the night porter at my hotel.'

'Tell me everything.'

'Adnan, his name was—why do I still remember that? I can't recall what *good morning* is in Hungarian, but I remember the name of this night porter in Cairo. Well, anyway, I stopped to collect my key, there was nobody else around in the foyer at that hour, his English was excellent, we got talking, and when I asked him if he was a Muslim or a Copt, he said he didn't follow any religion at all.'

'Unusual.'

'Totally unexpected. "What about life after death?" I asked. "Any views on that, then?" This was Egypt, after all. He pointed to my mobile phone, lying on the desk between us. "It's like this," he said. "When the battery goes dead, all you've got is this telephone. Nothing's *gone* anywhere—ring-tone, the list of missed calls—the phone is just dead." I remember staring at the phone for a moment, while he stared at me to see if I'd caught the drift. And I don't know if it was a *sign* or something, but the phone immediately started ringing.'

Silence. Amidst the roar and clatter of the highway north, there was a pregnant silence in our car.

'Well, who was it, then? Not Jesus, I hope. Don't tell me you got Jesus on the line.'

'No, it was Harvey Norman's back in Tweed Heads—the recliner I'd ordered had finally come in.'

'Ah.'

'You'd have liked Adnan.' No doubt, but she was veering away from the subject.

'Do we *fear* this sort of nothingness, though?' I asked. 'When you said yesterday it was death we're afraid of …'

'Fundamentally.'

'… fundamentally, yes, striving to ward it off by having mud-baths and taking some weird alkalising greens supplement with added vitamins every morning and so on …'

'That's not quite what I said, is it? Have you been taking supplements?'

'What I want to know is if you think people

commonly fear death as *nothingness* these days, since their religious imagination has dried up. Total extinction, like the phone gone dead. And, if so, why? Or do they mostly fear the run-up to death?'

'You mean, the broken hips, the strokes, the …'

'Yes, the dementia and painful feet. Nobody warned me about feet. On television people are forever running—have you noticed? Not just children, either. Do you know Larry David? He wrote *Seinfeld*. He's as old as we are, very frayed around the edges. Younger than thingamajig, the household name—Woody Allen—I suppose almost everybody is now, but all the same, ancient. The other day on television I saw Larry David running through Beverly Hills like a Zulu warrior. How is this possible? Is it a special effect?' Sarah smiled a little crookedly. She can't even walk without difficulty. 'Still confident about all those steps at Borobudur?'

'I'll take them one by one,' she said. 'How else? I didn't say I was confident. But to answer your question: no, surely not, I can't believe people fear nothingness these days the way they were terrified of hell in medieval Europe. Roasted over a fire for all eternity in blinding agony for nothing more than a spot of adultery—who wouldn't be scared shitless?' I got the feeling she was now briefly reviewing one or two of her own spots of adultery. I gazed out of the window and thought of Dante's hell, all nine circles of it, swarming with unrepentant sinners—heretics, sodomites, popes, usurers, adulterers—sunk in a sea of fire and boiling blood. Then Giotto's fresco of *The Last Judgment* popped into my mind. Same period—early fourteenth century. Once you've seen this extraordinary work with your own eyes—it takes up the entire back wall of the Scrovegni Chapel in Padua, glowing with gold and red amidst all the blue (the faded sapphire blue) above and around it, you are drowning in blue as you stare at it ... you remember it for life. Jesus in dead centre, welcoming the smug blessèd to life everlasting in paradise with one hand (no emptiness here, by the way), while sending the damned in a river of fire down to hell with the other. Here Lucifer squats awaiting them in his monstrous nakedness right at the bottom. We all stare in silence at this beast. What can you say?

'It's a long time since anyone has taken eternal damnation too seriously, surely,' I said. 'Or paradise, for that matter.' Not since a century or two after Giotto died, in fact, if Philippe Ariès can be trusted on the subject. Eternal damnation went out of fashion half a millennium ago in Europe and has not been replaced with anything you can visualise. Hindus have reincarnation, of course, as well as *moksha*, or release from the cycle of rebirth, much like the Buddhists' nirvana, but what this transcendent state of bliss actually *is*, nobody can know. Beyond time, beyond space, beyond family and caste and *things*, at one with the One Supreme Self, but very hard to picture—as it would be. However, for Europeans in recent centuries, according to Ariès, the afterlife is a blank.

An intriguing exception to this blankness is offered by near-death experiences. There's been a surge of interest in them since the mid-seventies in Western countries, especially in America, where educated people are running out of options. Typically, the shadow self (whatever it is—a soul, a force field) floats up to the ceiling and then down again to describe what is lying unseen on top of wardrobes, bookcases and even roofs. I shouldn't mock: some sense a divine presence while free of their everyday body, although I must admit that in the accounts I've read of near-death experiences the conscious self remains as much a part of the mortal, entropic time-space continuum as any body is. As a rule, they report, not a transcendent reality or oneness with Being Itself, but conversations with 'spiritual beings' and long-dead aunts. 'Experiencers', as they call themselves, include neurosurgeons, psychiatrists and Harvard graduates, they are by no means all the kind of gullible victims that charlatans commonly target.

What these reports remind me of above all is Enid Blyton's Joe, Beth, Fanny and Dick (now Franny and Rick) and what they saw when they climbed up the Faraway Tree to visit the marvellous lands in the clouds snagged at the top. Few experiencers report seeing anyone quite like Saucepan Man or Moon-face, let alone the treacle puddings, toffee shocks or peppermint creams, for instance, that Enid Blyton's children find themselves surrounded by in the Land of Goodies (so much sugar, but no sex, of course, the children being only five, so for them it's not unlike being seventy-five), but the sense of a magical, transformative adventure is the same, and at the end, like Blyton's children, the experiencers all get called home to tea. There is no mention of death in the realms they visit, as there is not in Blyton's lands at the top of the Faraway Tree, either, unless you count the fried fish (which I do).

No wonder the accounts sound similar: all the stories, Blyton's Magic Faraway Tree tales and the experiencers' reports, echo what's been called the monomyth (in Joseph Campbell's well-known formulation). Underlying just about every form of storytelling from Greek epics to Hollywood blockbusters, if Campbell was on the right track, you have: the questing protagonist, shaken out of his normal way of life by some disturbance, who strikes out, perhaps at the urging of some kind of mentor figure, on a journey to an unfamiliar realm. There he faces tests, battles enemies, questions the loyalty of friends and allies (and that's crucial in Blyton's stories), withstands a climactic ordeal, teeters on the brink of failure or death, and ultimately returns to where he began, victorious but in some way transformed.

The most famous convert of all to the idea of veridical near-death experiences, the American neurosurgeon Eben Alexander, describes being briefly dead in 2008, in a celebrated account now available in over forty languages, in terms almost identical to Blyton's tales of the goings-on at the top of the Faraway Tree. Alexander writes of feeling 'trapped in a dark space', surrounded by 'grotesque animal faces', and then being pulled up through a purple hole in the clouds into 'the strangest, most beautiful world' he'd ever seen, where he encountered 'a beautiful girl riding on a butterfly's wing' and a 'wondrous being who unlocks ... many secrets of the universe'. (Which are left unspecified.) Eventually they return to the dark space to find in place of the earlier grotesque faces the faces of loved ones. Nice. The experience has, as one investigator has noted, the advantage of combining what did happen (cardiac arrest, for instance) with what the dying man or woman would have liked to happen.

The similarity of the plotlines of such near-death experiences to Campbell's monomyth proves nothing, of course. Whether or not near-death experiences are the spasms of a brain shutting down, the oxygen supply choked off, neurochemicals rioting and the brain's temporoparietal junction going haywire, or proof that consciousness is, at the very least, not dependent on the brain (but engineered now in some electromagnetic clustering pulsing somewhere off to the side), nobody knows. How could you know? That didn't stop Oliver

Sacks, predictably, and thousands like him pouring scorn on the very notion. I have the feeling that near-death experiences will turn out to be the twenty-first century's version (more male this time, less theatrical) of spiritualism, replete with similar astounding claims of contact with the other side and strands of ectoplasm floating in the ether. In its day, spiritualism was also embraced and scientifically tested by chemists and physicists such as Sir William Crookes and by Sir Arthur Conan Doyle, who was nobody's fool, for all his eccentricities. Daniel Dunglas Home, another celebrity adept, did levitations for royalty. Yet where is spiritualism now?

The near-death phenomenon is currently being investigated with scientific rigour, as it should be. Be that as it may, the near-death plotlines and the remnants of religious promises of some sort of paradise aside, most of us in this day and age, suspecting the worst, have, I suspect, stopped picturing anything at all.

Medieval Europeans pictured the afterlife quite differently, as we know. One of the things that strikes you about Giotto's monstrous vision of hell in the Scrovegni Chapel in Padua is the feeling that he probably believed it was all more or less true: for Giotto, as for Dante, *extra ecclesiam* there was indeed *nulla salus* (no salvation outside the Church). The tombs of the righteous in the fresco are open and the souls in them, looking very like bodies, rise to heaven. The sinners tumble into the fiery abyss. How dispiriting, then—no, that's too insipid a term, but I can't think of anything appropriate with more punch— to see that 700 years later, amongst the vast throngs of visitors to the chapel from every country on Earth, breathless, all of them, with wonder, it's likely that nobody at all, not a single one, no man, woman or child from anywhere, now believes in the truth of what they are looking at on the wall of that chapel. There are still plenty of believers across the globe, but few, I imagine, in the literal truth of Giotto's picture of the afterlife, and fewer still with Giotto's frescoes on their bucket list. They're art now, they're heritage, but not thought to be literally true any more than Aboriginal myths about the origins of Uluru are. The virgin birth might still have some subversive attraction in the Western psyche, but not this ghoulish picture of life after death.

What we experience and desperately wish to hold at bay as death draws nearer is more a kind of horrified regret at being annihilated, I think, than fear of what will come next. There is, our culture seems to have concluded, no other reality but this one. Only cartoonists draw angels. From the back seat of the car, I studied the back of the Javanese driver's head. What the Javanese believe with confidence is anyone's guess. There was no point at all in asking the driver what he thought, as I might have asked a driver in Moscow or Tel Aviv: the question, as I've said, is a Western one.

No other reality but this one. It's a position many of us have slid backwards into, as it were (even the near-death experiencers), without considering the alternatives. Not even many clergymen, unless repeating comforting religious formulae during a ritual, will stick their necks out to talk about being dead. What could they say with any confidence or conviction? So what we fear these days is less likely to be unending torture at the hands of a psychotically vengeful father-figure than what Ariès calls 'the last convulsions of the machine that is breaking down'. Ourselves, in other words. It's not really the idea of post-mortem nothingness that is soul-destroying to contemplate, but rather the pain and parting just before we die. That is what half the developed world these days is trying to ward off: the painful falling-apart and the parting. For some the parting is even more unbearable than the physical suffering: I noticed an article in the paper recently about a young American woman called Elizabeth Holmes who founded a healthcare technology company aiming to help us 'elude death' as well as, more tellingly, to build 'a world in which nobody has to say goodbye too soon'. Forever, she means. She was a billionaire by thirty. Saying goodbye to the cat is shattering enough, let alone saying goodbye to those we love more than the rest of the world put together. The mere thought of it is heart-rending.

'And there's something else, too,' Sarah said, when I told her what I was thinking. 'There's something else we fear.'

'You mean the loneliness and boredom? Losing your mind and so on?'

'No, something worse than any of those things—nothingness, the fires of hell, dementia, bad feet …'

'What?'

'Tolstoy.'

'What do you mean—"Tolstoy"?'

'Don't rush me. It's on the tip of my tongue.' When you've recently had a stroke, a lot of things are.

'*The Death of Ivan Ilyich.*' It was surprisingly crisp once it came out.

I know Tolstoy's novella well. Nabokov called it Tolstoy's most vivid, perfect and complex work—or words to that effect. It isn't, but it's unforgettable, like one of those gruesome German fairytales—'Little Red Riding Hood', for example. It's a relentlessly joyless tale: a severely ordinary man, a provincial civil servant, is diagnosed with a terminal illness—presumably some sort of cancer, although we're never told precisely what it is. His mental and physical suffering are harrowing, and then he dies.

'I wouldn't have thought it would be your sort of thing at all, Sarah. So grimly Christian.'

'Yes, but he does see that great light just before he dies. That last chapter stays with you, doesn't it.'

'All that terror,' I mused, remembering, 'all that hideous pain, all that horror of death and the enveloping darkness—he suffers for months, lying there on that sofa on the brink of the abyss …'

'Yes, the sofa … dying on a sofa makes it worse somehow, don't you think? At least give the man a bed, I thought.'

'... and then, an hour before he dies, W*HUMP*! He's struck in the chest by that great bolt of something or other from the *beyond*, and gets thrown on his side the way you are on a train sometimes, when you think you're about to move forwards but instead you're shunted abruptly backwards.'

'And he hur- hur- hurtles,' Sarah says, smiling, 'into a vast black hole, a dark abyss, but suddenly, in the darkness, right at the end, sees an all-enveloping light. And he dies in a flash of light. There is no death after all. Just light.'

'Well, I'd call that a happy ending, not a nightmare at all, wouldn't you? A fairy-tale ending, really.' More Disney than Grimm.

'Or a bit Buddhist, no? I mean, since we're on our way to Borobudur ... nothingness as light.'

'You're in good company, saying that. Nabokov, from memory, thought the same thing. In fact, Tolstoy was a Christian at the time.'

'Anyway,' Sarah continued, feeling no compulsion to follow up on the details, 'there's something else in that story that's even worse than the fear of hell or nothingness, it's something nobody much ever mentions, yet ...

Damn!' She bit her lip and frowned in concentration. 'I've got the book on my Kindle, so I'll have a look later. I remember being bowled over by it at the time. Let me get back to you on that one!'

All thoughts of Tolstoy abruptly disappeared when, without warning, we swerved round the orange truck in front of us and swung off the road to the left into … in a word, Java. It had been there all the time, of course, a hop, step and a jump from the main road, hidden from us by the long, thin line, the endless line, unbroken since we'd left the hotel, of shops and warehouses, mosques and minimarts, crowding the roadside. We plunged into it. Java is green and watery. It is rice, corn and chillies in a checkerboard of mud. It climbs in steps, the Javanese countryside, ever bluer, and eventually a misty, purplish black, up into the roiling sky. To dive headlong into it like this, out of cacophony into silence, is to wake abruptly in an altered state.

For that matter, I thought, my eyes resting on the herd of doomed goats we were now edging past (*Idul Fitri* being only a month or two away), if you wanted to get metaphysical about it, what if *this* observable reality turned out to be, rather than the only one, just one of many that are the case? What if the universe really were not everything? Or, for that matter, what if it were nothing at all—of no substance whatsoever—while consciousness were everything? The men who'd built Borobudur wouldn't have batted an eyelid if I'd asked them what they thought about the proposition. The goats beside us would be finding out what the score was all too soon. I didn't bring it up with Sarah—it would only make her tetchy when she needed all the positive energy she could muster. For the present, for today, she and I would ward off decay and bad feet and the pain of saying goodbye forever to those we loved by plunging deeper and deeper into the startlingly green Javanese countryside, excitedly on the lookout for Borobudur. Somewhere nearby in all this vividly verdant, muddy wetness was the biggest stupa in the world, a triumphant explosion of beauty affirming that there are many realities other than this one. Indeed, this might be the least of them.

The stupa at Borobudur doesn't tower, it swells up out of the valley's steamy lushness like a massive upturned bowl, pinkish brown. All the same, the thought of climbing all the way to the top would daunt anyone but a child. Standing by my side at the bottom, Sarah looked as if she'd lost heart.

'I'm never going to get to the top of that, am I,' she muttered dispiritedly. 'What was I thinking!' In silence we watched the gaily clad crowds clambering up the steep stone staircase to the first gallery. (No one in black in Borobudur.) In silence we gazed up at the stupa's layered terraces, at the rising rows of Buddhas ringing this vast sculpted mandala crowned with three rounded galleries—at the scores of Buddhas, hundreds of them, circle after circle of carved Buddhas, rising up into the sky. There are meditating Buddhas, alms-giving Buddhas, teaching Buddhas, Buddhas turning the wheel of dharma and Buddhas hidden inside smaller stupas. Right at the top, piercing heaven, there's a bell, a huge, hollow, stone bell. Emptiness. (But not nothingness.) And, for a monument embodying the world's impermanence, I must say it's lasting well.

'There's a ramp over there, but it only goes as far as Desire,' said the guide, Mr Saliman, a slightly bossy man with a paunch and polished English. 'The lowest level.'

But still quite a climb. 'In Sanskrit *Kamadhatu*. *Kama*—you know, as in the *Kama Sutra*. Lust and passion, but also sensual enjoyment of any kind. That's the first level. To the higher levels there are just the steps. Ready?'

'Thank you, yes.' And off we set, a little unsteadily, but resolved. 'So what's above Desire?' I asked chattily.

'I shall explain when we get there.' Or *if* we get there, he was no doubt thinking. 'I like your sunglasses, by the way—very stylish.' He was friendly, but erratically.

In point of fact, Sarah made her way up the ramp with surprising ease. When she reached Desire, she was still looking quite sprightly. 'So green,' she kept murmuring, looking back down at where we'd come from, 'so incredibly green, almost a sapphire green, I feel I'm drowning in all the green.' Strictly speaking, she was sensually enjoying herself, although the pleasure of the eyes seems less reprehensible than other sensual indulgences. Only the hills to the west were darker—thickly forested hills that appeared to be slumbering, like a jungle-covered giant sleeping on his side.

We both liked Desire very much. 'In Indonesian we call it *nafsu*,' said Mr Saliman. We liked the word *nafsu* very much as well. 'Marijuana, massages, drunkenness, sex and gossiping—do you see? The reliefs are all showing these things.' In vivid detail. Faces. The procreating self, which after all, at root, is responsible for the whole orgy of appetite and depravity.

'What's wrong with gossiping?' Sarah wanted to know.

'Gossip keeps you attached to the world. In your religion also St Paul warned against it, by the way.'

'St Paul is not part of my religion.'

'Most of the bas-reliefs are hidden now, but you can see photographs in the museum. Murder, rape, abortion, also planned parenthood and some farming.'

'I see.'

'There are eight hot hells. Fishermen, for instance, are boiled alive for several centuries for killing animals. Also criminals are bound in searing chains.'

'What kind did you say?'

'Searing ones. Searing.' So even the Buddhists had something hot to fear in the afterlife. We took our time, but eventually clambered up to the next level: *Rupadhatu*.

'This is the Realm of Form. Also square galleries, you see? Square means the Earth. It's like Desire, but now the passions are under control,' said the guide. 'Form is still there, however. The self as form. Faces, you see, lots of faces everywhere. The life of the Buddha and other enlightened beings is also here. Please examine.' The passions are in abeyance at this elevation—in temporary disuse pending further enquiries, as it were. Devout Buddhists will make no further enquiries, of course, having their minds already set on pure knowledge. It sounds a bit like old age, really, I thought to myself, as I examined the bas-reliefs: fading passions and the mind, at least on its good days, drifting upwards to things it's hard to put your finger on.

'You're not yourself a Buddhist, Mr Saliman?' I asked after we'd walked around the first gallery of Form, slightly dizzied by the hundreds of carved panels in the walls.

'I am Muslim. But once the Javanese were Buddhists. A thousand years ago Buddhism was flourishing here.'

'So I gather. You're not attracted at all to the Buddhist view of the world?'

'No. Shall we go up further?'

'To Nirvana?'

'Not yet, more Form galleries first. Nirvana comes

right at the end.' He headed off up the steep stairs. 'Or so they say.' And for the first time that morning he grinned.

Panting and struggling a little with the steep stone staircase, which was crowded with scrambling children, I followed Mr Saliman higher. While Sarah stayed on the first level of Form to take another turn or two around the gallery, chatting to exuberant locals, the guide and I rose gently from gallery to exquisitely panelled gallery, until we reached the steps to Formlessness. I was not in awe—it was all too bewildering to seize my soul (not that Buddhists believe in essential selves), the universe it suggested too alien, too far beyond my understanding. Buddha bathed by the gods in a perfumed bath, Buddha as an elephant entering Queen Maya's womb—none of that sort of thing touches me, it is too outlandish and fantastical, too *foreign*; I'm no credulous pilgrim from the days of the Buddhist empires that ruled in the archipelago a thousand years ago. Nevertheless, I was drawn upwards to the rounded terraces at the top, to Formlessness and Enlightenment, although it feels more like falling upwards, upwards into bliss. 'Square is Earth, round is heaven,' Mr Saliman said gnomically. No statues of the Buddha up here, no faces, no forms, and consequently no *selves*—up I climbed to the base of the main bell-shaped stupa, piercing the sky at the mandala's pinnacle.

Nirvana. The 'ultimate up and out', as an American friend of mine, Ward Keeler, put it after an extended period meditating in a Burmese monastery. It's the only way out, in fact, for earthlings. And in a hierarchical society the way out is always up—as Ward, an expert on Buddhism and hierarchies, has pointed out.

'Nirvana is the great quenching, the joyful extinguishing,' Mr Saliman murmured, cryptically and little breathlessly once we'd reached the first circle, the square galleries now below us.

'Of what?'

'Of the three fires: passion, hatred and delusion. Of the delusion of a self. That is the teaching. The self is blown out like a candle. It gutters and goes out.' *It gutters and goes out*. What is left when that happens is not nothing, apparently, but something best understood as emptiness.

'So what comes next, Mr Saliman, when the enlightened person dies?'

'The Buddha didn't say.' Mr Saliman knew perfectly

well what happened next, so was unmoved by Buddha's silence.

The conundrum of how to be something and nothing at the same time just never goes away, really—after all, *something* is there, but not, it seems, what was thought to be there: that turns out to be nothing. *But if there is no self, whose arthritis is this?* as the Jewish joke about the Jewish Buddhist has it. Zinger! Sarah has a stock of Jewish Buddhist jokes. Buddhism itself doesn't have much of a lighter side.

The Buddhists first looked this puzzle in the eye 2500 years ago, and not much later, in Greece, so did Epicurus (who did not believe in an afterlife, only in disintegration). Then, in Rome, just before Jesus was born, Lucretius, prophet of the particle, who didn't believe in life after death, either, looked at the question of how to be something and nothing at the same time. Later, the Catholic Church, understandably, was aghast: the Catholic Church insists on essences and souls, having no reason to exist unless essences are real—well, there's the real estate, but apart from that. It excoriated Epicurus and his followers as whoring wine-bibbers. When Poggio Bracciolini rediscovered Lucretius in the fifteenth century, he arguably helped to set in motion the Renaissance and the growth of modern science. Particles, just electrically charged particles, as we now know them to be, with nothing ghostly floating in the interstices at all—that's the universe. I'm not sure the Buddhists even believe in particles, do they?

I craned my neck looking up at the stone bell soaring above me. 'The Dutch built a bamboo teahouse on the top of it in 1844,' Mr Saliman said. 'At that time the religious significance of Borobudur was forgotten.' I could have done with a cup of tea myself, to be honest. It had been an exhausting climb.

'So it's empty, naturally, this big stupa,' I said. It was a half-question. 'I mean, empty for symbolic reasons.'

'A Dutchman once entered it,' said Mr Saliman, 'and inside he found ...' He hesitated to let a group of chattering schoolgirls get past. What on Earth could the Dutchman have found? What can there be in any *sanctum sanctorum*? A void? A mirror? An image? What could the *non plus ultra* be? (And why am I forced to resort to Latin?) It's a question that has fascinated me for decades—in Egyptian temples, for instance, or at the heart of Hindu temples that I am forbidden to penetrate.

We know what is in the Holy of Holies in the Jewish Tabernacle, even if we may never set eyes on it: the ark of the covenant, covered in gold. Once the girls had passed, Mr Saliman resumed his tale: '... and inside he found a dagger, a gold coin and a small bronze statue, unfinished.' So in other words, money, a weapon and a face (if unfinished): pretty much the same at the top as at the bottom, after all. Isn't it always? As the Zen proverb has it, the only Zen you find at the top of the mountain is the Zen you bring with you.

It wasn't Buddha, Epicurus or Lucretius, by the way, who first opened my eyes to how threadbare the idea of an essential soul is *in the light of day*. I'd been familiar with the notion in theory from the esoteric Christian teachings I'd been following since the age of about ten, but it was the humble slime mould that brought the silliness of souls home to me, and it happened in a Chinese restaurant in Gundagai, of all places. At a table in the Chan Kong on Sheridan Street one evening half a lifetime ago, halfway between Sydney and Melbourne, in the middle of absolutely nowhere, I was abruptly brought to life by slime moulds appearing on the television set in the corner up near the ceiling. Yellow ones. God in heaven, it's a monotonous journey, that run up the Hume from Melbourne, stultifyingly dull and fawn and flat. The occasional dun-coloured hillock just makes it worse. In Australia your response to the rolling khaki landscape is a sure indicator of how *echt* you are as an Australian, how rooted you are in the sheep-shearing, sand and sunlight. The landscape tests your bona fides. I fail. By dinnertime that day I was desperate for something soul-searing to happen. Just five minutes into the program on slime moulds, I felt I'd been struck by a lightning-bolt of wonder. It was epiphanic. Once blind, I could suddenly now see. (Russians, of course, have a short, sharp verb for this phenomenon: *prozrel*. It means 'I saw through to what has been there all along'. In an instant I *prozrel*.) My view of the world and its possibilities has never been quite the same since Gundagai. I finished off my chow mein in a rush of exhilaration. It was like being twelve again. Slime moulds! Who'd have thought!

The astounding thing about slime moulds—and, as it happens, they are abundant in Tasmania, creeping slimily all over the forest floor within yards of where I usually sit to write—is that there is no mouldy *self* there. It moves with purpose, it solves problems, it searches for food (and loves cornflakes), zipping through mazes to get at food, it forages and spawns, it can even design road networks, and does a better job, in front of your eyes on YouTube, at planning a railway network for Tokyo than the Japanese engineers did. Yes, it's smart. Yet there is no 'it'. There's nobody home, no brain, no nervous system, let alone a mind or soul. Just a single-cell blob. Sometimes it forms an aggregate splodge with other blobs, as ants do in an ants' nest or birds do when they fly in a flock, but there's still nobody there, any more than the anthill or a flock of starlings has a transcendent self. At those times it's a self-organising system of aggregated amoebae, but there is no self. And it hits you that that's what 'you' are: a smart, self-organising system. And all those promptings from Epicurus and Lucretius, not to mention modern atomising thinkers such as Barbara Ehrenreich, are eclipsed by ten minutes of YouTube in blazing colour: you are an aggregated system. It hits you like a smackeroo blurdy. It doesn't mean that *nothing* is there, but *you* aren't. How bracing. (*What is missing from this picture?* Something is, I know, but what? I rather think it depends on the light you examine it in.)

Half an hour or so after we'd reached Nirvana we

arrived back at the bottom again, a little shaky from the descent, but buoyant. Sarah, with lots of help from other women, had actually climbed up rather higher than the first level of Form. 'Unforgettable,' she said, a little croakily, when I asked her if it had been worth the effort. 'I've been time-travelling! I've been to the ninth century and back! Not in a sound and light show, either, but the real thing.'

'How much did you manage to see?'

'I saw what I could.'

'You're not upset about only getting halfway?'

'I told you: I saw what I could. As you did, as a matter of fact, in a different sort of way. It's not a school assignment.'

'So how are you feeling?'

'A bit wistful.' And we both smiled. How could she feel wistful for what had never been? Yet she'd hit the nail right on the head. I felt oddly nostalgic myself, remembering what I'd never had but sometimes longed for. We trundled off with the guide towards the park gate through the dazzlingly green gardens.

'I was leafing through the guide book while I was waiting for you,' Sarah said as we walked. 'Not everyone agrees, you know, that Borobudur is a sort of three-tiered cake with Enlightenment at the top. There are newer theories. Various people in Berkeley, California, and so on have come up with stuff. Scholars, Sri Lankans.'

'Well, I like the old version,' I said. 'It feels right.'

Mr Saliman slipped the tip I'd offered him into his shirt pocket without looking at it, smoothly, as if nothing had happened. 'You don't want to exit through the bazaar, do you, as the locals do. So unsettling after what you've been looking at, so jarring. All those *things*!' He smiled again and gestured towards the entrance. 'Let me take you out by a quicker route ... for foreigners.'

Out in the car park the idea of extinguishing the self was less attractive than it had been on top of the stupa where the view was so uplifting and redolent of rare insights. After all, from a historical perspective, we'd only just managed to get ourselves a self, a self we can mould as we choose and not just as religion, class and custom dictated. These days it's all Jane Fonda yoga classes, selfies and years in analysis, but in fact that's new: we've been keeping journals, painting self-portraits, and writing autobiographies to record our distinct selves for no more than a few centuries. Thanks to the flowering of the market economy, not just knights and clerics can be singular in their outer and inner lives (how they used their talents and dressed, in their beliefs and secret thoughts), but everyone. Even some women, although few as yet in Java. So back on the ground at Borobudur the prospect of merging for eternity with a single, formless Super Self was fast losing its appeal. Why would anyone want to do that for more than a weekend these days? As we walked towards the market economy in full swing behind the rows of cars and coaches, the everyday world went off like a multi-coloured fireworks display all around us. There seemed to be so many things down here for a self to do.

'I can feel appetite drifting back,' I said to Sarah, looking about me with a touch of concupiscence and hunger. It was lunchtime and absolutely everyone was beautiful. The car park was a shimmering palette of lithe, glistening bodies in vivid colours, a hodgepodge of spicy smells—of succulent cuts frying in ginger, garlic, cardamom and coriander. The air was thick with *nafsu*.

'I never did get past appetite,' she said, fumbling in her bag for a cigarette, the very essence of unslaked desire and evanescence. She hardly smokes at all, but savours it when she does light up.

'Peckish?' I asked.

'Ravenous.'

'Good.'

We followed our noses.

No Place for Sissies

It's bizarre: there never seems to be anybody here. Where is everybody? In the rooms, if we care to look as we pad along the corridor towards Rita's at the back, there are sometimes wraithlike figures propped up in bed, snoozing or watching television alone, and in the Lounge there's occasionally a clutch of white-haired inmates playing cards or staring vacantly at the television set, but rarely. There's a quiz show on Channel 7 today, but there's nobody watching. 'Spin and sail! Let's play the game!' The screaming studio audience becomes orgasmic with excitement. We walk on in silence, along empty oatmeal-coloured corridor after empty oatmeal-coloured corridor. The rubber runner (quickly moppable, and that's important here) muffles the sound of our footsteps. Little hissing *whumps*, that's all you can hear.

Towards the back of St Ursula's it's quiet now except for Rita's neighbour's endless cry of 'Somebody help me, somebody help me', but nobody does. Nobody seems to have any visitors except Louisa, whose Down syndrome son is winding wool into coloured balls for her to knit with, but he's always in her room with her. *Why is there no one here? Why are these old men and women dying in a muffled beige void?*

When we get to Rita's room, right at the back of the building, we can see her sitting slumped in a chair in her dressing-gown. Her head is oddly askew on the pillow propped behind her white head, the eyes closed and the mouth slightly open. There's an uneaten custard tart on the tray in front of her. But when we go into the room and walk up to her to kiss her, she stirs and smiles at us: 'Mngk,' she mumbles, 'eat up,' and offers us the tart. 'Can I go home now?'

'How are you today, Mum?' Peter asks brightly.

'Isn't it *still* ... so *still*.' She sneezes exquisitely (*chink! chink!*) and sighs.

And it is still. The window looks out on the same empty inner courtyard, all paving stones and pots of unwatered geraniums. It's not empty of things, but of life. Once again, looking out at it through the venetians, at its emptiness and dryness, I wonder why places like this are all so cloistered, so inward-looking, so shut off from the world. This is a good place, too, this is a nice place, this is St Ursula's Grange, only the comfortably-off come here to slide downhill and die. The word Grange brings a clutch of thatched cottages in Hampshire to mind, a village like Nether Wallop where Miss Marple lives, but it isn't a village, let alone a grange, it's a nursing home, sealed off from the world. It's assumed you'll want to die staring at a pot of stringy geraniums in an empty courtyard. It's taken for granted you wouldn't want to cark it watching people go to work, walking their dogs, shopping, playing football or building an extension on their house. It seemed obvious to somebody that you'd want to kick the bucket in tranquillity.

Privacy is delicious sometimes, and a little peace and quiet at night is certainly an advantage, but who wants to be tranquil all day every day, for God's sake? You're about to be completely and irremediably *still* forever. In the meantime, why not live a bit? Make a noise. Wave. Tap your feet. Enjoy the world. Eat a sandwich out in the garden. Talk to passers-by. In his eighties, by the way, my own father (Da, as I called him) used to sit on the front patio in his Hawaiian shirt pretending to read his English-French phrasebook, engaging anyone walking past in a moment's light conversation—he wasn't many doors down from the shop (there was only one in Gerringong at the time), so he rarely had to wait long. Rita is in no state to eat a sandwich out in the garden, much less wave to passers-by: she doesn't eat much at all these days, she's shutting down, she's coming undone, she's little more than a skeleton with papery skin stretched over it, her breast barely rising and falling under her nightie. Her jaw sags and her eyelids droop. In slime mould terms, she is visibly disaggregating.

No, it's not the devil or nothingness or the cycle of rebirth we have reason to fear, I think to myself, as Peter takes his mother's frail, white hand in his. What we have to fear is this: fading away painfully, alone, infinitely bored and possibly incontinent, looking inwards at emptiness. Old age is certainly no place for sissies, as Bette Davis remarked. Institutions such as the Grange are fine for profitably processing the incurably old, but not for making their lives worth living out while they cling to consciousness. At least Rita is housed, I suppose, where someone keeps an eye on her. All over the country thousands like her live in doorways and under railway bridges. She gives me a surprisingly cheeky smile. 'Eat up, Olive,' she says, pushing the tart towards me. 'Not just now, Rita,' I say. She nods and dribbles. It's all the same to her.

I turn to stare at the geraniums again, splashing the lifeless courtyard outside with red. The wave of excited laughter from the television set in the Lounge only makes the underlying silence thicker. I suspect thick silence is the aim here. Why are we so obsessed with tranquillity, both outer and inner, at this moment in our society? In the face of eternal silence, I'd have thought that animation had more going for it, but it's tranquillity that has become a fad.

At one level it's understandable: cities are crowded and cacophonous places—there are just too many people on the planet, after all, over half of them squashed together in urban neighbourhoods—so the better-off either live sequestered from the city, walled off from it as stylishly as possible, or else move to the country to live more serene lives. If I lived in Dacca, Delhi or even

Denver, I'd probably hanker after a bit of peace and serenity myself, at least from time to time.

Inner peace is much prized as well, and were I a single mother of three I can imagine I might also prize it. But if you're not something of the kind, why would you? Inner peace is an even more faddish fantasy than seclusion. To be marketable, whole swathes of the population have to feel busy and stressed. 'I'm sure you must be very busy,' people who are about to ask a time-consuming favour write to me sometimes.

'No, not at all,' I say, as politely as I can, 'I just don't feel like doing what you want me to do.' The purveyors of inner peace don't like people like me. Inner peace is said to put us in touch with something transcending our everyday lives, something that makes us more creative, more ... oh, I don't know, more in touch with ourselves. The thoughtful yet busy look for inner peace on retreats, seek timelessness in mindfulness, and learn to chant with their hands held out, palms up, po-faced, to balance their chakras. In fact, you get precisely the same result from a glass of wine with friends, as Barbara Ehrenreich (microbiologist and political activist) has pointed out in *Natural Causes*—from intimacy, in other words, and sitting about pleasurably making conversation—but acupuncture and mud baths are more effective class-signifiers. Mindfulness was concocted in Boston, Massachusetts, along with Facebook, TripAdvisor and one or two other innovations now trending, by an entrepreneur called Jon Kabat-Zin, a Zen-trained psychologist who wanted Buddhism without all the spiritual, Buddhist clutter. Is mindfulness the ultimate Jewish Buddhist joke, then? Who these days does not have a little buddha on the mantelpiece? Or at least a pot-bellied figure of oriental mien smiling serenely at nobody and nothing in particular? Virtually every atheist I know has one. Even the hotel in the *kampung* where Sarah and I stayed in Java has two huge stone buddhas, relics from the days when Buddhists once lived in Central Java, one impassive white figure glowing in a niche in the garden and another by the lotus-pool in the restaurant. Serenity in stone. Spotlit at night, they are mesmeric in their allure and mystery. I never feel the one in the restaurant quite approves of us *relishing* anything, yet what else are restaurants for?

On the windowsill beside my desk at home I have a Ganesha, not a buddha, but my elephant-headed god is far from tranquil or impassive. Ganesha is never looking for repose. My pot-bellied, four-armed Ganesha is *dancing*, that's what he's doing, standing on one foot, fat and graceful, intensely alive, his trunk a bit shiny from where I rub it. There's something faintly lewd about him, if you look at him closely, he definitely has a Tantric side, although mine is not accompanied by the nude goddess he sometimes plays with. My Ganesha wants me to dance with him, not play dead.

Tranquillity is not a new obsession: Epicurus, two and a half thousand years ago in Athens, was convinced that, along with *ataponia* or the pleasurable absence of pain, *ataraxia* (impassiveness) was vital to any mortal's happiness. It's often thought that by *ataraxia* Epicurus must have actually meant something like the sort of calm so many of us seek in meditation or prayer—well, not Rita or Peter or anyone we know, but lots of people these days. A sort of stillness, in other words—a two-edged sword if ever there was one, but attractive in uncertain, narcissistic times such as ours. The Greek word that Epicurus used simply points to a freedom from disquiet or anxiety. What you do with this freedom is your business. The sort of calm the Virgin on the wall in the corridor outside appears to have achieved, for instance, is a permanent state of dazed melancholia—she is at peace, in other words, but, unlike Ganesha, hardly joyful. And most of the residents at St Ursula's look more becalmed than calm, more tranquillised than tranquil. Whatever the case, I am more focused on animation, on life as a dance, not on sitting cross-legged in meditation. Ganesha's mother Parvati is also famously a dancer, by the way: just picture the small miracle of the *nataraja*, for instance, the goddess poised mid-dance inside a brass circle, left leg raised across her body. And his father Shiva, Creator (and Destroyer) of the Universe, is the cosmic dancer, dancing inside an aureole of flames, dancing at the hub of eternity, long hair streaming in some cosmic wind and left leg lifted with infinite grace across his body, balanced on the demon Apasmara ... But what does any of this matter? It doesn't matter a jot, none of it is real (any more than chakras are) and none of it matters, but it gladdens me when it comes to mind. (And I must say I like the notion that Ganesha was his mother's son, but not his father's, since Ganesha was fashioned by Parvati from mud, without any interference from Shiva. Furious at being sidelined, Shiva cut off his son's head, replacing it with the head of an elephant. I wasn't made from mud, but I was also my mother's son, while Da was my adopted father, having no more to do with making me than Shiva did. Da approved of dancing. He bought me dancing shoes. And I started taking dancing lessons when I was about four.)

My eyes are fixed almost catatonically on the geraniums in the sun just outside the window when Rita suddenly says 'Isn't it still,' again with startling crispness. And it still is still. It's always still in here. Loneliness. While Peter strokes his mother's hand and smiles at her, I think about loneliness. 'Can I go home now?' she asks again.

It's the subject *du jour.* The British Prime Minister has appointed the first Minister for Loneliness—a woman, naturally, you wouldn't want a man doing it. On a recent television program about centenarians almost everyone complained of feeling lonely—not afraid of death at all, not one of them mentioned fearing death, but deeply lonely, even desolate. After all, almost everyone they once loved was either dead or deranged. In some cases, literally everyone, there was no one left at all. How do you arm yourself against that? Over the last ten years or so, especially once she was in her nineties, we've watched Rita grow slowly lonelier: eventually she had no visitors at all, her world had shrunk to her unit at Montpellier Gardens and its front porch, with no one left to play solo with on a Wednesday—or at least no *friends* left to play solo with. Once a week she came to our house to spend the day with us and the dog. Sometimes we drove down to the sea for a sandwich and a thermos of tea. And then she fell over. Who was it found her that first time? Maybe it was the helper—Maeve, I think her name is—when she came to give her her tablets.

That's the thing, Rita: you are catastrophically diminished. When you first moved into the 'village' at Montpellier Gardens, you used to make day-trips to the country or go out for a coffee with a friend; at first you caught taxis or buses into town to go shopping; then you stopped shopping and emptied your wardrobe and kitchen cupboards bit by bit of all signs of having had a life; then didn't go anywhere at all. A blouse or two, some slacks and shoes, a set of crockery for one, that's all that was left at the end … you didn't want to be a burden when you died. You once obsessively did crosswords ('What's the capital of Tibet?' you might call out from the couch. Or: 'How many m's in "Pomeranian"?') because they were widely rumoured to prevent the build-up of beta-amyloids in the brain and get those neurotransmitters really firing. Then you took to just staring out of the window at the weather. *Isn't it warm isn't it cold isn't it windy isn't it still isn't it isn't it …* then you hardly noticed what it was. You used to read shiny magazines about what film stars and minor royals had been up to, and then you didn't—you'd never really cared about what Angelina or Camilla were doing anyway, in reality nobody does care, it's never been of any consequence to anyone, least of all to you. You strode along briskly beside us for years on our afternoon dog-walks, you really stepped it out sometimes at the beach or on the track along the rivulet, then you started to dawdle, then dodder, then simply sat in the car as the sun went down while we walked the dog without you, and then finally you asked to be driven home instead of going anywhere with us at all. You used to cook, you were famous for your date loaves and Anzacs, now can't really be bothered to eat—half an apple here, a cheese sandwich there. You shrivelled. You became solitary. Then you fell over. Now look at you.

I'm not sure that Rita was ever self-aware enough to know that she was lonely—she thought she was just alone and depressed. She went more or less unnoticed, bored and in low spirits, even when her husband was alive—many women of a certain generation did, after all. Marriage is everywhere spruiked as a defence against loneliness, but it sometimes increases a man's or a woman's isolation in our individualistic sort of society. In Java life is unthinkable without a partner embedded with you in an endless network of family relationships. Even strangers are called 'father', 'mother' or 'brother'. Marriage seems not to be about your sexual likes or dislikes so much as a way of establishing an honoured place in your community, allowing you to have some self-respect. In India marriage is the only way of surviving for most people, especially, although not only, outside the cities. As R.K. Ramanujan put it in his hugely readable essay 'Is There an Indian Way of Thinking?' (and there certainly is), everyone is 'contiguous with the family' for their whole lives, there is 'no phase of individuation from the parental family' at any point in anyone's existence, as there is in Australia or America, an Indian life being made up of intimate interferences of a kind a Westerner would resent and take steps to put a stop to on the road to independence and maturity.

In our sort of society—less rural, more based on choice—marriage, it seems to me, is no guarantee of anything, not even of companionship. Not only does it often provide no balm for loneliness while it lasts, but with the cruellest of ironies, when it has indeed been a couple's main source of intimacy for decades, it may leave the survivor devastatingly lonely when his or her partner dies. The Grange is peopled by scores of these survivors, playing bridge on Thursdays with other devastated inmates whose names they can barely recall from week to week, otherwise watching television day after day, night after night, in a room full of plastic flowers, until they shut down completely, defunct at last. Deceased, dead as a doornail. 'Pushing up the daisies' is what Da, who dropped dead mowing the back lawn one afternoon, usually called it, but that makes it sound a lot jollier than being dead probably is.

So what can we do about being alone and loneliness? 'You have to practise being alone,' my old friend Katharina said a few weeks ago in Berlin when I asked her that very question. In her eighties now, and divorced, she's worked in old-age care in Sydney and Berlin for as long as I've known her and lives happily alone—or, rather, with a good friend: herself. She's gaunt but full of life.

'It's an art. And you have to start practising *early*!' I did, I think. Although, to be honest, I'm not sure. I'd always like to have someone close by to kiss my soul, someone I'm joyfully intertwined with. How else can I put it? Not, of course, that I believe in souls. Katharina certainly began practising early, I know. When we first met on a train in Sri Lanka, she with her silent husband Erich beside her, me with just my suitcase, she was already practising hard to be alone, I could tell straight away. This tall, thin German woman was friends with herself—you could feel it from two rows back on the other side of the carriage. And that's the point. Now forty years later there we were making soup together in her tiny kitchen, high above a small lake in Charlottenburg. Forty years! How inspiring! Peering down at the lake that sun-splashed afternoon in early November, I wanted to soar up into the sky and then plunge down into the explosion of fiery reds and yellows that the lake (a palette of deep greys and blues) was almost lost in far below us.

'Yes, you must practise to be happy alone,' she said, adding a large pinch of paprika to the steamy mix. 'And the key to being happy alone—what I think—is friendship, intimate friendship, *Innigkeit*.' I liked '*Innigkeit*': a warm closeness with someone's living inner world. 'That's what unlocks you,' Katharina went on, 'opens you up, frees you: friendship between hearts. But it takes a lot of practice. And it's a two-way street, by the way: you have to be worth befriending.' My memory of the precise words Katharina used that afternoon in Berlin is shaky, but I recall those words very clearly indeed: 'you have to be worth befriending'. Has Rita been worth befriending, being intimate with? I look across now at her pale, dry face. What could anyone have intimately befriended? Rita has never had any intimate friends in the three or four decades I have known her, just family and the odd card-playing companion while living in Montpellier Gardens—the home, the village, the community, whatever Montpellier Gardens calls itself—someone to take the bus into town and go to Myer with. There was Olive, I suppose, for whom she seemed to have a genuine, if shallow, affection. She did like Olive, but it wasn't intimate. For a start, Rita has never befriended herself. If all your self-respect was crushed out of you in childhood, that's going to be difficult.

'So often have I seen it,' Katharina said, stirring gently. Such a beautifully simple silver ring on one long finger. 'Finnish,' she said, when I asked about it.

'So flat and watery, Finland, but so stylish. I lived there once.'

'*Ach so,*' she said. 'That must have been before we met.' We bounce around like this a lot. I only mention it because it's what happens when two people with inner *sweep* meet up. Many find it irritating, but it's the price you pay for a talkative inner life. One moment it's spices, the next it's Finland, and before you know it it's St Bartholomew's Day, Greek verbs and wombats. We never mention Hitler. 'Yes, loneliness,' she said, looking for the cheese to grate into the soup. 'Almost every day where I worked—can you believe that? *Unglaublich, nicht wahr?* But it's absolutely true—almost every day one or other of the residents would say to me: "I feel so lonely." And I would often think: *Natürlich!* Of *course* you're lonely. You're empty inside. What is there in you to grow close to? And now it's too late.' The staff in old-age facilities are rarely syrupy and sentimental.

We were rather quiet, I remember, as we ate our soup, following the trails of the various conversations, often *tête-à-têtes*, going on in our heads. Then, just before she took the dishes back to the kitchen, she said: 'It's not that you have to know all about volcanoes or Thomas Mann or have been married to a famous poet or even travelled a lot or collected butterflies or … anything like that, really …"

'No, of course not.'

'… it's that you have to be in a conversation with yourself about things that matter, things with roots. Can I say that? Your inner world has to be like a room full of conversations others will want to join—although you can just sit and listen to them alone if you want, that's fine. Yet the room is so often empty, once you've got past the usual banalities about the weather and their sore backs. But if someone's eighty-eight, what can you do?'

Katharina seems never to be lonely—if truth be told, I'm slightly envious; I'm not as happy alone as she is. Over the years, both before and after her divorce, I've watched her grow close to a young Greek couple (restaurateurs in funky Kreuzberg, a vivacious couple—she *loves* them and they love her), I've met her lifelong friend Brigitte, and there's also Hannah (she flies to Chile to see Hannah all the time) and her brother Klaus (and his dog—they have her heart), there's her paramour Luis in Hamburg ... these are just the intimate friendships I know of. And inside Katharina, although she's no intellectual, there are voices speaking in German, English, Spanish and Greek all the time, about things that are beautiful and deeply human. She's never read Heidegger or, for that matter Proust—who has? I haven't, either—but she's read a thousand others, she goes alone to symphony concerts once a month, travels far and wide to see exhibitions from around the world ... she's polyphonic, too blithely so for some, no doubt, but at least there's a finely tuned inner life there to be intimate with. As in that train carriage in Sri Lanka all those years ago, you instantly sense a conversation or three or five going on in her that you want to eavesdrop on or join. And so, when she offered, apropos of nothing at all, to fix the broken zipper on my suitcase that day half a lifetime ago, I smiled and thought: *Warum nicht?* And look what happened. (I should have said 'Why not?' more often in life, that's obvious.)

※

'You're talking to yourself,' says Peter with one of his grins, not realising how apropos his remark was. Berlin vanishes in an instant—*pfft!*—and I'm in Rita's room at St Ursula's again. As always, there's a faint smell of lasagne hanging in the air. I do talk to myself sometimes, when I'm trying to nut things out, trying to find the right words for something, even in the street. Have I been muttering *Warum nicht?* and *Innigkeit* while standing staring at the geraniums? Am I going gaga myself?

Not all conversations will make loneliness bearable, not by a long chalk. For a start, they have to be conversations between two people who care intensely about something—not everything, but *something*, something bigger than their own welfare or fetishes, something magnifying, even the broken zipper on a fellow traveller's suitcase is a start, it doesn't have to be rainforests. In one of those mournful Swedish reveries of Ingmar Bergman's from the fifties—in black and white, as I remember, about old age, loneliness, death, God, and time coming to a stop (about your life and my life, in other words, any thinking person's life in old age)—someone says (and perhaps it's the main character, the ageing, deeply likeable, but lonely professor, a widower, travelling to Lund to receive a prestigious award) that loneliness is the punishment for not caring enough about others—in his case, being too cold and selfish. I must think about this. Here in Rita's room, in the midst of this totally silent explosion of deep feeling and regret, I keep staring out at the sun-baked courtyard, as still as stones, and know I must think about this. There's something in that movie about conversation itself, too. (The movie was called *Wild Strawberries*—such a sentimental title, isn't it, really, the strawberry patch from our childhood garden remembered in old age.) Right at the beginning of the movie the professor says that he's given up on 'social intercourse': it's mostly just gossiping about and passing judgment on the neighbours' behaviour. So he has withdrawn from nearly all social relations, and feels lonely in his old age as a consequence.

Nowadays, in the era of social media, as often as not, conversation is shallow gossip, not about the neighbours, but whatever strands of trivia float to the surface. It's like listening to geckos *chichukking, chichukking* around a light-bulb.

A few weeks ago, as a matter of fact, I took a five-hour train journey through country New South Wales. Behind me were sitting two amiable older women, unacquainted until the moment they found themselves sitting beside each other. They chatted amiably for five hours about their children and grandchildren. Neither was remotely interested, needless to say, in the other's children or grandchildren, yet that is what their amiable intercourse consisted of: an exchange of footling information about people who didn't matter to at least one of them, chatter so weightless it evaporated instantly like steam from a kettle. Taree, Gloucester, Maitland, Newcastle, Gosford ... on and on it went, mildly pleasurable to both of them, blandly warm-hearted, as the mildly picturesque countryside drifted past the window ... Fiona's lovely home near Penrith, the grandchildren's schools, Mark's divorce, young Kyle's football prowess, all relentlessly of no account, an endless rack of *prêt-à-porter* views and storylines. They moved on to arthritis at one point and thickening toenails, but drifted back to families. There was just one token sideswipe at refugees. ('Oh yes, I *know*.') It was life as seen on television all day and all night: sport, bodies, families and food, over and over again. Food, families, bodies and sport. Nothing much to nurture an inner life.

Beside me on the train that day a woman was reading *Better Homes and Gardens*—or was it *Home Beautiful*? Anzac caramel tarts, how to fix bad breath, plants for the bathroom. *Things*. And why not? She also appeared amiable, and we, too, got chatting in a neighbourly way about absolutely nothing at all (one of my skills). She did, however, have a deeper, caring side, offering me a brochure to read entitled 'How to Make Friends with God' just outside Dungog. But I couldn't care back.

In this connection something from *Mrs Dalloway* is floating towards me out of the distant past ... the movie, I think, not the book, because it's Vanessa Redgrave I can see taking shape in my mind's eye. Like *Wild Strawberries*, Virginia Woolf's novel is also about death, ageing, suicide, belief and unbelief, but not with any mournful cast to it. It has *éclat*, this movie—not to mention Rupert Graves, Michael Kitchen and Natascha McElhone. Someone mentions that conversation seems so easily to turn to 'vapid chatter', a phrase that has stuck in my mind, like Vanessa Redgrave's marvellous face. (She's had cosmetic surgery on her forehead, but nothing else. A smoker's face. She doesn't mind looking old, I read somewhere, but is careful not to look 'scruffy'.) Chatter is worse than chat, of course. Chatter is mostly noise. It's prattling, jabbering, gibbering and waffling on. Chatter is not *meant* to add up to anything. It's barely intercourse at all.

Rita didn't chatter, she chatted, but it was rarely conversation, and never intercourse. She cared deeply about nothing and nobody but the man now holding her hand—and even then not really about his inner world, the things he loved and believed and longed for. I look across at her in her recliner as she takes her hand from her son's and reaches across to finger her custard tart. 'How are you, Olive?' she asks.

I know what this place smells of (apart from lasagne): boredom. The merest whiff of boredom chills me to the marrow. The prospect of enforced boredom in old age dismays me more than the threat of pain, it panics me like the thought of being buried alive. Rita has been bored for fifty years, bored to the bone, bored *white*.

This whole place reeks of a boredom so profound I can barely breathe sometimes. Everyone is drowning in it—well, not the Tongan nurses, who are always *jolly*, eyes wide open, nor Eddy, who is on stage and moisturised every second of his working day, but everyone else. Indeed, here's Eddy now, sweeping in from the wings. 'But we haven't eaten up our custard tart, sweetheart!' he coos. 'What will we do with you?'

'I want to go home,' Rita mumbles.

'Of course you do, sweetheart! All in good time!' He straightens her blanket and fiddles with the blind. 'How about a nice cup of tea?' With a flourish he conjures the tart away, pirouettes and disappears. A sickly silence settles on the room.

'Somebody help me!' croaks the woman next door.

I feel a spurt of queasiness and take a deep breath to ward it off. Tedium—the deadliness of a becalmed old age—is on my mind at the moment. Before I boarded that train to Sydney (such a boring name 'Sydney', by the way, such a blunt and shut-off sort of name, like Chris Lilley's Dunt) I'd spent a weekend with a couple I know in one of those dullish, closed-off communities circling a golf course near quite a gritty riverside country town.

Milder climes tend to breed this sort of settlement. Stands of eucalypts, empty, clean streets, empty front gardens, bland lookalike houses, all dark grey or beige, showing no sign of life. Deep silence and unbroken seemliness by day and by night as far as you can see. Occasionally an expensive car will sail silently by, the ageing driver, in sunglasses, staring straight ahead. In four days nobody (men on their mobility scooters, women dead-heading the roses) so much as nodded at me. Only the lorikeets and galahs were busily and noisily alive at dusk. Where the hell *was* everybody? Why was everyone practising being dead? I suddenly missed Calcutta (as Amit Chaudhuri spells it). In Calcutta you are intensely, fiercely, extraordinarily alive. Calcutta is a nightmare, Calcutta is a vision of the end of the world, but it's never boring. We have forgotten how to be alive.

Whether the bored are aware of it or not, boredom means there's nothing happening, and you don't know when you'll be able to leave. A small desert island, if you're alone on it, or an airport lounge when a flight's delayed, are quintessentially boring. So is childhood, from some children's point of view, and so, from my point of view, was this community bunched around a silent golf course (for all the shiny four-wheel drives in the garages), marooned in a sea of unending sameness. *Nothing is really worth doing when you're bored,* that's the point. When you're bored, you don't know what you want.

'Can I go home now, Olive?' Rita says when our eyes meet. Dear one. Something crumples inside me. Death's vestibule is comfortably appointed, but it isn't home. God save me from ending up somewhere like this. I want to end up at home. But where is 'home'? Not, of course, in my case, whatever I might say, in Calcutta.

※

Back from Borobudur at the hotel in the *kampung* that afternoon in April, dizzy from the muggy heat, Sarah went off for a siesta while I trailed across the lush, damp lawn to the pavilion where drinks are served—a bar, but not the kind you prop yourself up at. This bar is a graceful Javanese *pendopo*, a small, tiled platform with a pitched roof balanced on slender posts, beside the old fishpond of the original Buddhist villagers. You lounge, chatting idly to whoever is relaxing there, or else, alone, your mind floats off into the surrounding greenery, threading its way between the trunks of the palm trees. After days of heavy rain, you can sit comfortably, sipping something refreshing, marooned in a shallow sea of muddy water that stretches as far as you can see. You wade back to your room. Heaven.

Not far away, the village's main street cuts straight through the middle of the hotel, between where I am sitting and the office and restaurant. I am at peace, but the village is going about its business: children cycle slowly past, as do old men, a car or two goes by, ducks scurry about like tiny startled nuns, someone somewhere is sawing timber, and all around me, out of my line of sight, villagers are talking, cooking, eating, carrying, selling, building, washing, hoeing, planting and fishing in the streams that flood sometimes, leaving us to wade to our rooms, to the restaurant and to the pavilion I am sitting in. It's not that villagers are 'busy' in a Western sense, it's more that they have a place in the overall picture of activity. A village is quiet but alive. Here the quiet is shattered several times a day by the call to prayer—so few houses, so many mosques. Without the call to prayer time would evaporate entirely.

It was a village Da lived in towards the end, now I come to think of it, a string of cottages on a hill above the sea, a real village, with two small churches, a post office and a general store smelling of biscuits and haberdashery—not quite a Javanese or Indian village, needless to say, not a *kampung* like the one the hotel nestles in, but a village rather than a town. What a quaint word 'village' is! Before she came to the nursing home, Rita, too, of course, lived in a 'village': Montpellier Gardens. But it wasn't a real village—almost (a picturesque tangle of dwellings tumbling down a hillside like Da's village), but not quite. And there were no gardens. Apart from anything else, in Rita's 'village', everyone is old. Who first came up with the idea that the old want to live with a crowd of other old people? Why would they? As a rule, the old don't even much like the old. And you can see why. Like anyone else, the elderly like all sorts of people for all sorts of reasons. There's a competing myth that the young value the wisdom of the old while the old delight in the companionship of the young. Fiddlesticks! 'As a rule,' Bernard Berenson, the noted art historian, wrote in his diary at eighty-three (in his odd English), 'the young ones care not for our conclusions regarding our experience. They want their own and blast the consequences. So youth and crabbed age had better keep apart, except of course when youth has something to get out of age, and stimulates age by its acquisitive eagerness and zest.' Given Berenson's fame and wealth, it's not hard to read between the lines here. He quite fancied the idea of a disciple, as many older men do, but in real life it mostly turns out to be theatre. All too often what he calls 'impudence and bluff' take over and friendship does not develop.

Needless to say there are lots of things about traditional villages that I'd find difficult to live with—and Sarah, for example, would I'm sure find utterly impossible. As dyed-in-the-wool middle-class Westerners, our 'villages', the clusters of like-minded individuals we move amongst, sprout more in our heads than in the countryside.

In the Javanese *kampung* the doors are mostly wide open, day and night, the curtains rarely drawn. On my evening walks I would peer in while the villagers, who knew precisely how I fitted in (or didn't), would peer out. Everyone—the cook, the timber-merchant, the batik-maker, the imam, the hotel room-boy, the woman who rents out rooms in her cottage, the rice-farmer, the teacher, the schoolboy on his bike, the man who sells soft drinks in the market, *everyone*—has a place in the mesh. In the commonwealth of the righteous (the *ummah*), that goes without saying, but also in the tightly knit web of this small *kampung*. It defines him, moulds him, as it does his wife. Social relations, as the anthropologists like to say, are at the heart of everything. Every man, woman and child I see go past is true first and foremost to the village. (Sarah and I are true to *ourselves*—or at least we are on our good days.) Nobody is alone, there are no outsiders, and if one or two of them occasionally feel lonely, they would be unlikely to mention it to anybody, since feeling lonely is a failing. Mavericks and freethinkers mostly move into town. It's medieval, really, reminiscent of some twelfth-century French hamlet, but it has advantages over the modern city for those with little social capital: in the city the truck-driver and street-sweeper, the bricklayer and bicycle-repairman will be atomised, they will not even be ants in an anthill, just disaggregated particles in an organism so vast the mind cannot encompass it. Uprooted from the village, the lower classes—the labourers in the fields, those who work with their bodies rather than their minds—find themselves without a living self.

There is no context to have a living self in. You are your job (if you have one). In the city—any city, anywhere—those of us with some social capital are therefore keen to display it whenever we can to avoid being mistaken for peasants or workers: we buy our gluten-free bread at farmers' markets, jog along main thoroughfares or right through city malls, do yoga to tone our bodies (as well as our minds, we hasten to add—or not our *minds* as such, since minds, like germs, are going out of fashion, but our breathing and our *atma*), and insist on ethical chocolate.

Isn't there something between the city and the Javanese or Indian village, I wondered? The Romans, according to the classicist Mary Beard, herself unforgettably idiosyncratic, if her television programs are anything to go by, were rather in favour of diversity in their towns and cities, but at the same time of cohesiveness. In other words, a diverse but connected population. The Romans wanted everyone to 'join in', Beard says. Not everyone's cup of tea, of course, in this individualist era. As far as I'm concerned, joining in goes against the grain. I actively avoid joining in anything. Once long ago, I remember, arriving alone at a gay resort in North Queensland, I went to lunch alone, although not lonely, and sat by myself at a table for two at some remove from the other tables, looking out to sea. No sooner had I ordered the gazpacho than a lesbian appeared beside me, pressing me to join 'us all' at the group table by the pool. 'Oh, look,' I said, glancing across at the merry, topless throng, 'I've just got here, I might just sit by myself today and gaze at the waves.'

'Oh but you must join us,' she said, her tone hardening.

'Thanks, I said, but not today.'

'Oh but we're all one big family here,' she said.

'I hate families,' I said. (Well, I was working on a book on André Gide at the time. *'Familles, je vous hais.'* 'Families, I hate you.' *'Foyers clos, portes refermées, possessions jalouses du bonheur.'* 'Your homes shut off, your doors firmly closed, your possessions under smug and jealous guard.' And I do indeed shrink from families. In my middle-class Western fashion, I prefer all affinities to be chosen ones, as it were. My family, like my village, is in my head. It's kith for me every time, not kin! So I ate my gazpacho alone. I was, understandably, never invited to join anyone else again.

Is there perhaps a middle way?

Sarah didn't reappear for dinner after the trip to Borobudur. Borobudur had done her in. But the next morning, when she joined me for breakfast under Buddha's disapproving eye, she looked remarkably jaunty and refreshed in *vieux rose*.

'*Selamat pagi!*' she greeted me, shaking out her red napkin. 'Well, I've been rereading *The Death of Ivan Ilyich*.' She was hardly faltering at all today.

'And were you bowled over again?'

'I certainly feel as if I've been punched in the face by it, but that's not the same thing, is it. What a sparkling morning!' She smiled brightly and looked across at the shimmering lotus-pond. 'A coffee would be …' She swivelled to hail a waitress. 'Anyway, it's come back to me—the thing that's worse than nothingness, damnation and dementia.'

'I'm agog,' I said, spearing some papaya. 'What is it?' Tolstoy isn't breakfast fare, and I wasn't at all in the mood for him, but Sarah was eager to tell me.

'Well, Ivan Ilyich, you'll remember, is lying on that sofa in unbearable pain, tortured by all the usual things.

For a start, by terrible loneliness, he couldn't be lonelier if he lived at the bottom of the sea, as he puts it, or deep inside the Earth ... *at the bottom of the sea!* ... do you remember that line? I felt asphyxiated just reading it. He's surrounded by *people*, people everywhere, although nobody, not even his wife or children, *cares* about him, nobody touches him—I mean, puts out a hand and touches him—or pities him, nobody opens up his heart to him ... well, that's what loneliness means, I suppose: that nobody cares about you, nobody opens up his heart.' A pause to nibble a rusk. 'Or *her* heart. But women are thin on the ground in this story.' I remembered Rita saying years ago, when she first moved into Montpellier Gardens in her mid-seventies, that she longed to have someone touch her, just touch her, because nobody ever touched her. Not kiss or cuddle or even hug, but touch. We touched her, but not enough.

'And he's tortured by the *falsity* of everything and everybody, too, the veneer of lies. Why will nobody, not even the doctor, come out with the truth? Why won't anyone tell him he's about to die? Why can't anyone voice their real feelings, mention the emptiness of the lives they all lead, these city people, uprooted from the soil—is "soil" the right word?—not empty of *things*, of course, but of some other kind of vital awareness.'

'That's what clouds the spirit, isn't it, for Tolstoy: living in a world of mere things,' I said, aware as I said it of how many 'things' I'm surrounded by myself. 'He liked bodies, though, didn't he, old Leo—thighs, hips, strong legs—quite a lot of haunches in *Ivan Ilyich*, did you notice? Bit of a one for calves as well, Tolstoy. But not things.'

'Every last word and gesture, he realises, is geared to cover up the truth about life and death.'

'Like television. Have you ever watched that show …'

'He's also crushed by God's cruelty, God's absence—he feels abandoned, although, to be picky, it's he who's forgotten God, not the other way around. All anyone will really think when Ivan Ilyich finally dies is: "So what? Ivan died. I didn't."'

'So what is more frightening than pain and abandonment and the abyss?'

Sarah paused, then said very quietly: 'It's suddenly realising, at the point of death, that you've been dead all along. A living corpse, a tale told by an idiot, signifying nothing, and so on. It's seeing at the very last moment that your whole life has been "wrong" (that's the word he uses), a sham—not even evil, just empty, but not in a Buddhist way, of course, at least I think there's a difference, but a trivial way, a strangely eventless way'—Sarah was speaking rapidly now, she was in full flight—'your life will leave no trace at all, it's been spent indulging ordinary appetites, reupholstering your ordinary furniture, bickering with your ordinary wife, doing an ordinary job every day amongst ordinary people … And nothing can now be done about it. It's too late. Ivan Ilyich was given something beautiful and fucked it up. Ivan's whole life has been a lifeless life, a living death—and realising this as you begin to topple into the blackness is what's terrifying. Becoming aware that you've been dead since you were fifteen.'

'Fifteen?' I was curious to know why Tolstoy had chosen fifteen (if he had).

'Since adolescence, anyway, since your childhood came to an end. Tolstoy seems to have believed there's something genuinely good and joyful about childhood, something that is then corrupted and lost.' Another short pause as her coffee was brought to the table. 'I don't feel as if *I've* been dead since I was fifteen, by the way. Do you? Do you feel your life has been a sham?'

'No, not in the least! In fact, although I can't climb mountains any more or run for the bus, I don't think I've ever felt more alive in my life.'

'I feel much the same. Well, the stroke's been a bugger, but apart from that. Inside—you know what I mean. Why is that, do you think? What's our secret?'

I cogitated on this for a moment. 'The magic formula for growing older well? I don't think there is one.'

'Perhaps it's more of an art,' Sarah said, dabbing at her lips with a batik napkin. 'Is there a trick to it, though, I wonder, or do you just have to be born with the knack?'

'I don't know, but one trick is to never *quite* grow up in the first place. But I would say that, wouldn't I.'

PART II

Ace in the Hole

'I'm just a kid again doing what I did again ...'

'The idea is to die young as late as possible,' Ashley Montagu, the American-British anthropologist, quipped, but what exactly he meant by this witticism is unclear to me. I like it all the same. I like a lot of things he has said. Anyone born Israel Ehrenburg who changes his name to Ashley Montagu catches my attention. In point of fact, he changed it to Montague Francis Ashley-Montagu, which is even more sensational. Robert Zimmerman changed his name to Bob Dylan after trying Elston Gunn, but neither name has the flair of Ashley Montagu. Ashley Montagu died very late indeed (at ninety-four), but how young he was I don't know.

Did he mean that the idea is to die youthful-looking

and still frisky at a venerable age or just young at heart, still *feeling* frisky? Was that the same thing as 'failing to quite grow up'? Sarah had not been the first to accuse me of failing to grow up—earlier in the week in the pavilion—but who had been the first? I could hear her voice quite clearly in my head. Sharp, assured, not unfriendly, yet at the same time she'd hardly been patting me on the back. Yes, I can hear the voice, I can feel the faintly barbed edge to the words … not cruel, it wasn't meant to lacerate, but it *was* meant to jolt me. *You've never quite grown up, really, have you*. On reflection, I indeed hope not.

Up to a point, when the chips are down, you have to grow up, that goes without saying—one day you have to marry, or at least get sexually involved with, *someone* and apply for a mortgage and get old. It's not Neverland out there, after all, it's not all fairies and pirates and little boys flying about like birds, it's real life. To be quite honest, on the subject of the boy who flew about like a bird, 'the boy who wouldn't grow up', I must admit I find Peter Pan brattish and creepy. He would not allow himself to be touched, for instance, not even Wendy could touch him, let alone Captain Hook, and he seemed to still have his baby teeth at the age of fourteen. This is grotesque. Peter Pan is not at all what I mean by not growing up.

Ping! It was Caroline Baum who said it. Who else takes that tone with me? We're in a packed tent at a muddy festival somewhere, talking about a recent book of mine. Everything's smelling of mud. Mud and sea-spray. *You've never quite grown up, really,* she says at some point in the conversation, *have you.* The audience is delighted. *She's nailed him!* I am dumbstruck. What on Earth can Caroline mean? I'm over seventy, yet at this moment my age in years is quite obviously beside the point. Does 'not quite ever growing up' mean staying green, raw, and unripened forever? Wilful, solipsistic, naïve? I'm hardly innocent. Ogden Nash flashes into my mind again, some quip of his about how you're only young once but can stay immature indefinitely. Pithy as ever, but he made it sound like a ploy. My own failure to mature (if I have indeed failed) doesn't feel like a ploy. Is it an embarrassing blunder on my part? An oversight? Is it (God forbid) *gay*? And at what age precisely does Caroline think I'm stuck? Fifteen? Might I, if adroit enough, turn it to my advantage? Should I put my hand up to it?

'Sarah,' I said a day or two after we got back from Borobudur, 'what did you mean when you said that I'd failed to grow up in the first place?' We were marooned in another vast traffic jam, in front of a *warung* selling tea and chicken noodle soup this time. A small, thin boy eyed me from the doorway, sucking on a bright-red lolly on a stick. Thin, not slender. I stared back. He was unmoved. From that doorway there was, after all, an infinity of things to stare at that morning. It wasn't Hobart.

'Did I say that? Oh, I'm sure I wasn't being serious, my dear, just teasing you.'

'It's just that you're not the first to say it. In what way have I not grown up?'

'Pay no attention. I was just joking.'

'I'm curious. Is it a good thing or a bad thing?'

Sarah smiled, slightly aslant—we were both askew from browsing all morning in the heat amongst the bustling street stalls on Malioboro Road. 'Well, I wouldn't say it's either good or bad. I'm tempted to say there's wisdom in it, but I can't because you didn't *choose* to stay ... well, you haven't stayed a *child*, have you, so that's not the right word at all ...'

It's a word people sometimes use, though. It can be a compliment of sorts: I remember the painter John Olsen's son saying of his father in a documentary about him that that he was 'childlike in old age', that his fragile exuberance, even towards the end, was like a child's. And, speaking of painters, three months before he shuffled off his mortal coil, Thomas Gainsborough wrote a note to his friend Thomas Harvey, using a slightly different word: he joked that ''tis odd how all the Childish passions hang about one in sickness ... I am so childish that I could make a Kite, catch Gold Finches or build little Ships.' He was sixty-one at the time, suffering from a misdiagnosed swelling on his neck, not yet aware that he was 'sick unto death', as the Bible has it. The word he chose for the passionate delight he took in play—the playful pleasure Gainsborough took in the world—was 'childish'. 'Childlike' sounds much more endearing than 'childish', but the important thing at the heart of both of them is the love of play. Indeed, if John Cleese (born Cheese) is to be believed, without a child's love of play to no practical purpose, without a childlike curiosity for its own sake, creativity just can't take root. If you cast your mind back to Monty Python or *The Goon Show*, you can instantly see what he meant. If it's ever to flower it needs time as well, of course, time as a buffer from work. Cleese has no objection to work at the right time in the right place—in fact, work is the culmination of play for Cleese, it's where his play becomes art. What's vital for Cleese is to switch back and forth between play and work. Needless to say, Cleese doesn't work in a Chinese button factory. I wonder if he liked Fellini's *8½*. That's a movie about childlike, even childish, play culminating in a work of astonishing invention: a movie—the movie you're watching. Only the gentry can play all the time, it seems, having others to do their work for them. The result of playing all the time is Bertie Wooster. P.G. Wodehouse was creative, but his creation, Bertie Wooster, isn't.

During the decades between adolescence and retirement, the house-and-kids decades, you're only supposed to play at prescribed times: on Saturday afternoons, for instance, at tennis, or on Thursday evenings at potting or speaking French. You might even take on a mistress (on Fridays at five, *par example*) or climb Kanchenjunga with a bunch of enthusiastic trekkers. To play is to rehearse being deeply *you* at a given time in a given place, as even your dog knows by instinct. Once your time is your own again in your late sixties, on the cusp of being old, after years on the treadmill, going nowhere, you can play whenever and as often as you like: something in you begins to sing and dance *for the sheer pleasure of singing and dancing*. 'The advantage to growing old,' Quentin Crisp observed (tart to the last), 'is that you are towards the end of a long run and you can over-act appallingly.' Clearly, anyone who's anyone has been *acting* all along.

It's true: I failed to learn the rules. I have played all my life, failing to stop on reaching manhood, when you're supposed to take life seriously. I did get married and build a house, but it was a performance, not quite the same thing it was for the man next door, shall we say—I can see that now. I began to earn my living as a teacher (still performing with relish) and eventually came out as a performer, performing openly once a week on national radio. Whether in rude health or suffering like Gainsborough from misdiagnosed swellings, as it were, sick unto death, it seemed, too, once or twice, I kept on playing—with some flair, if I say so myself.

Men who do grow up play manly sports if they want to play at something. These days even women play manly sports. I never played manly sports. At school, it's true, they forced me along with scores of other boys unsuited to the game to play rugby, but I failed to take rugby seriously, scoring tries against my own team and constantly finding myself 'off-side' (whatever that might mean—I never discovered). Instead of learning the rules of rugby or running about the field shouting huskily like all the other boys, my friend Edward and I stood about discussing seriously life-enhancing things such as *The Goon Show* and Nietzsche. (Nietzsche, incidentally, associated old age with clarity of thought. It is the young who are more likely to be befuddled, in Nietzsche's opinion. It's worth pondering.) Edward was a German Jew and had plenty of opinions on Nietzsche. Our conversations were play of a far higher order than rugby. Edward did go on eventually to be a real man, by the way—someone has to, I recognise that, or society would seize up. A man works, only a child just plays.

Nietzsche, as it happens, also thought in terms of men on the one hand and playful children on the other. 'In every genuine man,' he wrote, 'a child is hidden that wants to play.' (*Im echten Manne ist ein Kind versteckt; das will spielen.*) My playful child, on the other hand, if indeed it is a child, is out in the open, not hidden at all. I do things (learn languages, write, read, converse, travel, flirt, dally, amble and promenade) at certain times, in certain places, according to certain rules, for the pure pleasure it gives me. Like anyone else, I have goals when it suits me (work goals, nesting goals, health goals), but I play more than I would if I wanted to be a real man.

The miraculous thing about play, though, is that it is never futile. For ten minutes, half an hour, half a lifetime, while you play, being alive is not futile. Your job may be repetitious and cosmically superfluous, the cosmos itself, for that matter, may be as random as the Irish National Lottery, but play itself is never meaningless. Nor is buying a ticket in the Irish National Lottery. From a child's point of view, every day is brimming over with things to give it purpose, for a child being alive is never pointless. And then most of us grow up.

Do I actually want to be one of Nietzsche's *echte Männer*, one of his grown-up real men? No—to be frank I don't, and, in any case, it's too late now. I don't see my failure to reach adulthood as a defeat, either. I feel now as if I have survived, almost unscathed, the running of some gauntlet or other—blow after blow after blow. I see failing to grow up as a kind of victory against a certain everyday way of being a man—a clock-bound way, measured out in stages, swathed in duties and achievements, ticked off one by one, before the final slide downhill into the usual dribbling nightmare of crossword puzzles, broken hips and daily incontinence. Everything about that kind of manliness strikes me as timed to perish before your eyes from year to year (and finally month to month)—the vigour, the virility, the power, the gait, the stance—in the lead-up to final shrivelling. You can't hoodwink death, that's clear, but you can decline to join the conga line dancing to its door.

I am not a child, in a hundred ways I am not a child (I know too much for a start, am too self-possessed), yet I can see what Caroline and Sarah mean: I haven't grown into *real* manhood. I do not want to own or control or spawn or take responsibility for what I do not love. Although it's now late, I do not want to stop playing with my friends in the field behind the house and come inside when called. Time is endless out here, you have no sense of it at all. I want to keep playing with panache, poetry and skill, together with an awareness of my roots. And so, when I am called, I usually find a way to dally.

One day I'll topple over the edge into Tolstoy's black hole—of course I will, as will everybody else—but I know the shape and colouring of the multitude of days before the end will be entirely different if I can just hold on to what was vivifying and pleasurable about being a child.

To be scrupulously honest, I am little drawn to actual children any more than they are to me. In true childlike fashion, it's the child in *me* I like letting out to play, perhaps with the child in you, but not with your children. For my taste, children are too self-absorbed, too credulous, too feckless and too impatient to endear me. It's enchanting to be a child, but the child's instinctive 'Me First' credo is tiresome in other people's children. As the British literary figure Diana Athill wrote at ninety-odd, as deliciously forthright as ever: 'It's hard to feel more than a vague goodwill towards anyone else's child.' That's it in a nutshell.

On the other hand, when you're a child, each day is an adventure, lighting up with flashes of wonder at what you've just discovered about the world. A child is curious—about everything from mucus to Mars, although, as I recall, with little empathy. (That comes later.) A child digs, invents, experiments and sticks things in its mouth. It's this curiosity about the world that 'binds you to life' when you're old and need binding, as Gide wrote in the book he was still writing the week he died, if you can manage to keep it alive. (Difficult at the very end, he said, when one's appetite for almost everything has waned dramatically.) Even boredom can be exquisite when you're a child, just time going at a snail's pace with no sign of a break in the monotony. And for all your bouts of loneliness when you are young, of feeling unnoticed and unloved by anyone at all, you have moments of giddying intimacy as well—just a few, but you do. Although you don't know it at the time, you won't have many like them ever again.

Yet I am not a child. Almost, but not exactly. I'm curious, I grab at intimacy if it's offered, even for five minutes, I thirst for adventure, I am curious for no reason, I haven't quite grown up, but I'm not a boy, I'm a man. I know too much. Over almost eight decades of reading and talking and thinking and travelling to know this world, I know far too much, from too many angles, especially about the human heart, to be a child. I am a hundred times too knowing.

Yet, paradoxically, one of the things I know—and can see that I know, now I'm near the end—is that I know *nothing*. Not in the sense that Manuel claims he knows nothing in *Fawlty Towers*—'I know nothing, I know nothing, I know *no-thing*, I am from Barcelona'—but literally *nada*. Well, not literally, but I do literally know as good as nothing. I think, of course—that's my saving grace. My mind is forever moseying around the agora, chewing over what it's just heard someone say—the perfume-seller, the clerks, the priest or Socrates, whatever catches my ear—and then it thinks. In *Wild Strawberries*, towards the end of his long drive to Lund to ceremonially receive an honour for his fifty years of academic research, Professor Borg falls asleep and dreams he is being examined on his knowledge. Through the microscope he's offered, he sees nothing, of the words written on the blackboard for him to interpret, he understands not one, when asked to diagnose a patient, he finds her dead, only to have her wake up suddenly and laugh at him. His impassive examiner finds him 'incompetent'. He thought himself wise, but he knows nothing, *nothing at all*. Still, Borg thinks. The dream seemed to make Borg a little melancholy, but he was Swedish. I feel a kind of euphoria. It's not unlike the jubilation I felt on the morning I abandoned the academic life. That was (briefly) like ascending into heaven.

'Kid,' said Sarah suddenly, as we pulled up back at the hotel.

'What?'

'Kid. You're not a child, but sometimes you're a kid.'

'Not bad,' I said, slowly nodding, and easing myself out of the car. I haven't sprung out of a car for years. 'Yes, I like "kid".' It's got the whiff of mischief about it. Larrikinism, by way of contrast, doesn't attract me at all—men behaving like ratbags in rowdy mobs and then going home for dinner leave me cold—but mischief has infinite possibilities. Once you grow up, though, mischief is rarely an option. Behaving badly is just about all you're left with, and that's not the same thing at all.

'Kid' ... I immediately thought of an acquaintance of mine, a middle-aged Californian named Boris, who keeps travelling (almost fecklessly, to be honest) around the globe, completely alone, achieving nothing but happiness. I was curious about why he did it. 'I guess,' he said over fish and chips by the water after a whole day doing nothing in a hundred different ways, 'because when I travel I'm just a kid again.' Doing what he did again, singing a song. Pure Doris Day, but the word is exactly right.

If you're serious about wanting to be a kid again, you must sing, there must be music, there must be a patterned performance of some kind to brace the soul, to give the heart muscle. John Olsen's son, I remember, in the documentary about his father said he 'sang', but his music was for the eye rather than the ear, it was colour. Kandinsky was in the air, unsurprisingly, along with Klee, at East Sydney Technical College where Olsen studied in the 1950s. 'Colour is the keyboard,' Kandinsky wrote in that influential little book of his, *On the Spiritual in Art*, 'the eyes are the hammers, and the soul is the piano with many strings. The artist is the hand that plays, touching one key or another, to cause vibrations in the soul.' Nicely put. (A touch too nicely, perhaps, but why be picky?)

The point about Boris is that he doesn't leave home aiming to learn anything (although he does) or to gain anything or discover anything (even paradise) but just to be a *kid* again. He doesn't just want to explore Rajasthan or the Bungle Bungles but to be a kid again in Rajasthan or the Bungle Bungles.

'Is there anywhere you *can't* be a kid again, Boris?' I asked.

'In Singapore, maybe,' he said without hesitation, throwing a chip to a seagull, 'and Minsk. You been to Minsk? It's Singapore without the food and the shopping...' He shuddered ever so slightly, although the breeze off the water wasn't cold. Crowds of seagulls were now homing in on us, squawking loudly.

'What about ... you know ... *here*, Boris?' (I like saying 'Boris'.)

'*You* can't play up here so easily because it's home, but I can. That's why I'm being a kid again here, while you have to go to ... where did you say you usually go?'

'Java.'

'Java. Right. Sounds steamy. Steamy is usually good.'

I considered the seagulls. It's uplifting and encouraging—inspiring, as people used to say until recently—to find a man Boris's age eagerly drawing close whenever he can to the things from his youth that make him glad to be alive! Scraping the dross of adulthood off them, burnishing them and freeing them to frolic in the sun.

It's particularly encouraging in a man as uncomplicatedly grown-up and middle-of-the-road as Boris is. Except when he's travelling, he could be anyone.

Later in the afternoon in the pavilion, watching guests and staff pick their way across the flooded lawn (it had been raining cats and dogs since lunchtime—raining tumultuously, with a roar, as it never does at home), I said to Sarah, who was enjoying a frozen mango margarita: 'Do you think that failing to grow up might be a mainly ... well ... *gay* thing to do?'

'It's hard to think of a man who's still a kid who isn't.' I could see her riffling through a list in her head of men she knew who'd failed to be completely grown-up as I had: her art dealer ... her Darlinghurst hairdresser ... her Pilates instructor ... the guys who ran the cabaret across the laneway from her house (they were forever bursting into song—quite literally) ... none of them children, but often kids again. Which is why she liked them. Women tend to, but it's a mistake to marry them, unless you have an understanding. I should know.

'There must be some, mustn't there,' she said. 'Why wouldn't there be? Byron, maybe, Casanova, the odd king of England ... whatshisname who married Wallis

Simpson, for instance. The only candidates who come to mind are aristocrats, though, the sort of men who never had to work.'

'The Duke of Windsor was royalty, strictly speaking, not an aristocrat.'

'But he didn't have to work—that's the thing. He just made whoopee, as far as I can see, and shot things.'

'As did Wallis Simpson, come to think of it. Or did she not even hunt?'

'Women … women …' Sarah said, picturing whole galleries of women she had known, 'I think women do it differently.'

'Do what differently?'

'Fail to grow up.'

'How?'

'I'm still thinking about it. But an ordinary man with a wife and children, a regular job and a house with things to fix in it can't afford the luxury of turning into a kid again. He has to grow up when he's about—oh I don't know—twenty-five and stay grown-up, get a job, put food in people's mouths. He can't go gallivanting about the place, staying out all night, popping over to

Paris on a whim, staying in bed all weekend if he feels like it.'

'Twenty-five? That sounds a bit early to me. A lot of men stay kids until much later than that, surely.'

'Thirty-five?'

'Even forty-five. In some cases you really can't tell until he's forty-five.' In other words, not so very long before his dick goes limp at fifty-five (as Google predicts it may well do). In my case, you could tell much earlier than that.

Most men who fail to grow up may well be gay (who knows?), but not all gay men fail to grow up. In *Less*, for instance, the prize-winning comic novel by Andrew Sean Greer about (amongst other things) being gay and not so young any more (fifty, to be precise, like Boris), even gay men seem to fear they won't be able to afford to stay young forever. A man Less (the titular character) meets in Paris on his farcical world tour as a literary nobody having a last stab at being a literary somebody remarks that he feels as if he's just understood how to be young. 'Yes!' Less agrees. 'It's like the last day in a foreign country. You finally figure out where to get coffee, and drinks, and a good steak. And then you have to leave. And you won't ever be back.'

'You put it very well,' says Javier.

'I'm a writer,' Less replies, 'I put things very well.' He does, too, but he's wrong. Quite a few of us have found a way to come back often.

Javier has bought a stake in a particular kind of gay world in which his worth depends on being sexually attractive to desirable men and not on much else. (Sound familiar?) It's fun while it lasts, but it doesn't last long. Once you start to sag in that world, la-la land just won't let you in again. Some gay clubs in Paris start shutting you out at thirty-five for fear you might dishearten the clientele. Few straight men, however, seem to care if they're attractive or not, once settled with their spouse and progeny, despite the herculean efforts of magazines like *GQ* to convince the world they do. Straight men seem to want to make an impression, it's true, they like to catch the eye, but take it pretty much for granted that being desirable is just part of being a man. Straight men seem more interested in *mattering*.

In urban settings these days, many gay men have more play time and more play space than most men do to perform their inner lives in. If they're astute enough, as they grow older they'll find they have less need to outgrow the kid in themselves—the playful, theatrical, mischievous, curious, flirtatious, inventive, risk-taking, often silly *kid*. After all, they're not headed anywhere. Life doesn't need to be linear, and they can stand aside from the cavalcade of their fellow humans marching, marching, endlessly marching forwards from birth to death.

In recent years, in more and more Western democracies, gays have been rushing to join the cavalcade, eager to lead a life 'like everyone else's'—to get married, set up house, have children, work hard, relax a bit and then die, taking the odd gay cruise up the Danube to recharge their boyish or girlish batteries. To be different, but also the same, nestling inside the common symbolic system of marriage and family. Who can blame them? But there's a script to be followed, if you want to be like everybody else. It has a beginning, a middle and an unbearable end.

Chichukking chichukking. The day was deepening into evening now, and the geckos were appearing, murder on their minuscule minds. Brutal little beasts, geckos.

Ruthless. *Chichukking* ... ZAP! I sat and watched Sarah picking her way across the lawn past the pond towards her room for a snooze before dinner. The steep roofs of the old village houses making up the hotel were glowing a dying-rose brown, each tile a finely etched burst of pinkish earthiness. Sarah turned into a mauvish silhouette against the lamp-lit walls across from me and was then swallowed up in the shadows.

I fell to pondering, as the frogs started up in the lotus-pond across the road, the question of how women play at being kids again. Take Barbara, for instance, my old friend Barbara, who has been writing about Javanese performance for forty years, and growing old with great brio, I might add, the art of it coming naturally to her. The thing is this: Barbara, although all her life an academic who took her research and teaching very seriously indeed, doesn't seem to take *herself* so seriously, having learnt how to play a little bit *all the time*. Many women, it seems to me, have this knack. (Like the flock of black cockatoos outside my window as I polish these lines: stripping bark off the tree by the front door, screeching joyfully, squabbling, mucking about for the sheer hell of it. The eagles circling outside the kitchen window never play. They watch and wait and then plummet earthwards for the kill.) And so Barbara has no need to overact outrageously on Fridays at the Flamingo, or be a kid again at the football once a week on Saturday afternoons, scrapping with all the other kids and stuffing herself with donuts and lukewarm meat pies. Like many other women, she doesn't need an excuse to act up. She catches gold finches and builds kites and little ships every day, as it were, like Gainsborough. Where men try to seduce, women flirt.

'Can I get you a beer, Mr Robert?' Klemen, a Christian from Makassar, is rapier thin with a boyish smile. This is a small farce we go through every evening.

'You know perfectly well I don't drink, Klemen.'

'But beer is not drink, sir.' His smile is slicing straight through me. 'I think gin is drink, no? Whiskey also.'

'*Meskipun demikian, Mas Klemen*—even so, you will have to tempt me with something else.'

'The usual?'

I nod. Why not? I watch as he slowly prepares the usual concoction. There's a courtliness to it here, as there would not be in a more time-bound society where we scurry to impress others. It's slowness, not briskness, that is a sign of dignity here—even of worthiness. I study him with quiet pleasure. One day Klemen will be somebody's undoing.

Barbara plays at being a kid again in another, very particular way, too: with her grandchildren. It's an intimacy that quite a few of my friends are passionate about: a Danish friend of mine, Katrine; Jenny in Yogyakarta; thrice-married Suzy; and half a dozen others. Indeed, Suzy calls it 'the greatest love affair of all'. I'd never paid any attention at all to grandchildren, barely knowing the names of even my closest friends' grandchildren, until Barbara said one day as we sat talking about the advantages and disadvantages of old age over dishes of ice-cream in the Chocolate Monggo café near her hotel: 'I think grandchildren are the best thing about growing old.' I hardly knew what to say, and so spooned in more ice-cream. I always feel slightly irked when people with children or grandchildren tell me—and you'd be surprised how often it happens—that having children is the best thing about being alive. I'll never know. It's like telling a blind man that the only thing worth doing in life is looking back down at the world from the top of Kanchenjunga. But Barbara would not have spoken with the intention of hurting me. So I just said with mild surprise: 'Really? The *best* thing?' Since she's known me for almost sixty years, she caught my tone.

'Sorry, I only meant ...' (flustered, she giggled and toyed with her scoop) '... you know ... for *me* it's the best thing about being old. For you it's probably ... Actually, what is it?'

God knows. Not giving a damn, probably. 'Are the grandchildren a stab at immortality, perhaps? A little bit of you going on forever.'

She thought for a moment, smiled to herself, and said: 'Not exactly, no, not immortality. That sounds to me more like grandfathers than grandmothers.' Barbara is very clear about what she thinks, but sometimes zigzags her way to putting it into words. 'You'll think I've gone soft in the head, but when I'm with my grandchildren I feel I'm being invited into their world as their equal ...'

'... for the day ...'

'... yes, for the day, or even just the afternoon. It's magic.'

'So you're one of the gang. It sounds like Enid Blyton.'

'Yes, I'm one of the gang, in league against the world,

including Dad and Mum. We share lots of delicious secrets we never tell the grown-ups. I'm a little girl again, we're all equal, I'm not necessarily even *head* girl. Best of all, though, they're not my responsibility—that's the thing! I love it, there's nothing like it.'

No doubt. We sat and savoured this, doodling with our melting treats. For me it was as fantastical as Narnia. Silence. 'What do you actually do when you're together?' I asked. 'What do you play *at*?'

'Oh, it could be sticking things in albums, or it could be building something with Lego or we might open a shop on the front verandah. Didn't you like playing shop when you were little?' (Well, I did, but had no siblings or grandparents, so I never had any customers.) 'Sometimes we put on little plays together for their parents, especially if it's someone's birthday. We put on *Harry Potter and* … the something or other last time, all squeezed into twenty minutes. But best of all is playing school, with me as one of the naughty pupils.' I was silently envious. This was play at its purest.

'I can't think how to put this without sounding a bit pompous,' Barbara said, readying herself to zigzag closer to the target. 'My grandchildren are no guarantee of immortality, but they do give me a chance to redeem myself, if that makes any sense. To start again. Well, not really, but it feels like that. They've taught me to wonder again at all the *small* things in the world—the shells and spiders and beetles and buttons and pebbles, all those things you find in rock pools and behind the back shed. I can sit in a tram the way they do and look at all the people around me—the faces and clothes and gestures and accents—with a kind of wonder. So it's a reprieve, do you know what I mean?'

'Yes,' I nodded, but only half did. I scraped at my bowl.

'It's not immortality, you see, but it is the feeling that I'll be remembered well beyond my lifetime. I don't like to think I might be thrown on some trash heap of memory when I die.' There, I have to say, she quite lost me. Why would anyone give a fig about how they might be remembered? When he was asked in an interview what he'd like his legacy to be, Gore Vidal replied without hesitation: 'I couldn't care less.' Still, people do care. At least Gore Vidal had the consolation of being remembered while he was still alive.

'What about men?' I asked. 'Do you think many

men would agree that being a grandfather is "the best thing about growing old"? I don't know many men who would tell me honestly if they did or didn't.'

'At home I'm not sure, but here in Java grandpa's job is to pass on the important stories to the grandchildren—or it used to be—the traditional ones everyone needs to know and take seriously in order to grow up. Repositories of ancient wisdom and so on: the older you are, the wiser you're supposed to be.' We both laughed, since that was obviously nonsense, and gazed out at the bustling street. 'Even at home I think grandpa prepares kids for growing up. Grandma, on the other hand …'

'Grandma learns from the grandchildren.'

'Something like that, yes.' We sat sucking lime juice out of long, cool glasses.

Nobody can play at being a kid again non-stop, obviously. Who would want to? Some things, especially at work, demand our solemn attention. I take those I love seriously (our lives are not just a Punch and Judy show) and the miracle of our planet very seriously indeed, but I suspect that over the years I have failed to take myself quite seriously enough to be like the man next door and the man next door to him. André Gide (who enjoyed being a kid again more often, probably, than he should have, especially in Morocco) also failed, and possibly for the same reason: he lacked a proper, grown-up sense of *time*, he wrote (his italics, not mine) in his final mischievous memoir, *So Be It*. Without this everyday sense of time, there is always a loss of seriousness, a swerve towards 'untimeliness' in your actions, 'untimeliness' being in Edward Said's opinion right at the core of 'comedy'. Not only that, Gide 'never succeeded completely in believing in the outer world'. I know exactly what he meant: you are sensitive to the outer world, but floatingly, sometimes puzzling over who exactly is dreaming whom, *because you lack the feeling of time*. Clock-time is essential to growing up. And so Gide could be many ages every day, not just an adolescent, say, or a man of eighty. 'It is only with great difficulty,' he wrote in *So Be It*, 'and very rarely, that I manage to be the same age every day.' And that, I believe, is partly why he had such an astonishingly good, quite fiercely serene, old age. Bravo!

Yutori

A beautiful old age is impossible if you don't clean up your clutter: clutter kills—cluttered time, cluttered space. Apart from anything else, it triggers cancer, Alzheimer's and irritable bowel syndrome. I read it in a newspaper in a teahouse near the Sultan's palace. Was it the *Jakarta Post*? I would swear by the *Jakarta Post*. The article was by an Englishwoman who'd read an article about how clutter kills by someone else in another newspaper altogether. Without a moment's hesitation, this Englishwoman had hired a professional declutterer to empty out her house. Now she had not just no juicer or batik tablemats, but no books, no CDs, no bread-making machine, no Mother's Day cards from her children and only one plate per family member.

It sounded pretty good to me (especially the bit about

the bread-making machine), if a touch extreme. Was there a middle way? I'm partial, naturally, to middle ways. Couldn't I ditch the Royal Doulton dinner-set, for instance, but keep the djellaba I bought in Fez? Just to bring back memories of the bazaar. And does Dostoyevsky have to go? I can't imagine ever deciding to reread him, I don't like being hectored, but a civilised bookshelf should have *Crime and Punishment* on it.

'Of course there's a middle way,' said the man sitting across from me when I mentioned what I'd just been reading. Young but already gaunt. Appealing. German? 'It's called *yutori*. Have you heard of it?' I hadn't, of course. '*Yutori* is the new mindfulness but much more fun. You should try it.' A smile I liked—not mindful at all.

'Why? What is it?' And, for that matter, I thought, why am I always the last person to hear about these things? I'd only just got a grasp on *wabi-sabi*, and now here was this new sensation from Japan that makes embracing imperfection old hat.

'I doubt there's a single word in English to cover it,' he said, stabbing another prawn.

'There often isn't,' I said, 'look at "Blitzkrieg", but we usually get the picture. Tell me more.'

'This table,' he said, 'is an example of what it is not.' I eyed the clutter crammed onto the table-top between us: cups, glasses, dishes of uneaten food, paper napkins, bottled water, tiny saucers of sambal as well as my copy of the *Jakarta Post*. 'As is this whole *warung*, by the way, everyone jammed in cheek by jowl like this.'

'Aha,' I said.

'*Yutori* means not being cramped.' I could hardly remember not being cramped by something—desire, obligation, schedules, goodness. 'It means having the time and space—and even the resources—to do, with a sense of ease, whatever it is you'd like to do. Plus a bit. That's the important part: *plus a bit.*'

What flashed into my mind immediately was the sort of scene every episode of *Grand Designs* finishes with: a couple with children called Granville and Clementine, sitting in an aircraft-hangar-sized atrium, staring up at floor upon floor of bedrooms, boudoirs, bathrooms and walk-in closets reached by a hand-crafted spiral staircase, looking trapped. They have all that room, yet are strangely hemmed in. By debt, by deadlines, by the need to own an architectural masterpiece and at the same time love it. Plenty of space but still no real *yutori*.

'Surely all anyone needs,' said my companion, 'is enough room, money and time, and enough knowledge as well, to be who we'd like to be. Enough plus a bit more to cushion us. Elbow-room.'

'Aha,' I said again. In a word, *Lebensraum*.

'Do you agree?' The faintest of five o'clock shadows.

'Well, I … um …' I said.

'Enough room, enough money and enough time—above all enough time—plus a bit. But not empty time. We need to live lives that have a bit of *Spielraum* in them, a bit of looseness. Do you say "play-room" in English?'

'I'll certainly say it from now on.'

'Our lives should not be too tight-fitting,' he went on.

'Japan is quite tight-fitting,' I said. As was his T-shirt, in point of fact.

'So I guess it's the word for what they want but haven't got yet.'

'Do I have to take classes?'

'No, you just do it.'

'No need to meditate or buy a mat?'

'No mats, no meditation.'

It sounded like just my sort of thing—a very middle kind of way indeed. I could feel my whole body relax at the mere idea of it. I resolved to start putting this *yutori* business into practice immediately, less (to be frank) in the case of our ceramics collection or our library than of my time.

At the airport the following afternoon, for instance, having got there a little earlier than I needed to—just fifteen minutes earlier, à la *yutori*—I simply sat and looked about me at what everyone else was doing. I looked across at the batik shop, the chocolate shop, the foot reflexology studio (a fixture at all Indonesian airports) and I noted the piles of Mark Manson's *The Subtle Art of Not Giving a F*ck* on a table outside the bookshop. (I was mildly surprised the local religious authorities didn't give at least a *small* f*ck about the public display of books with *F*ck* in the title, but I'd read the book and, on reflection, didn't give a f*ck myself whether they did or didn't.) I let time pool around me, there amidst the clutter of the Departure Lounge (the carry-on bags, the backpacks, bottles, children, rubbish, the endless signs forbidding things, the scrolling screens and the truckloads of useless gewgaws crowding the souvenir-shop windows). I simply floated quietly, but not emptily, in my pool of awareness, exactly as Hans had encouraged me to do. (I think his name was Hans—it was hard to read his scrawl on the napkin from the *warung*.)

When you're young, you have goals and rush headlong towards them, anxious to achieve, attain, take possession, be productive, win. Of course you do, it's the same all over the industrialised world: you have to eat and pay off the mortgage. Ogden Nash summed it up nicely: 'I would live all my life in nonchalance and insouciance, were it not for making a living, which is rather a nouciance.'

At my time of life, however, you see little point in speeding anywhere: it's rootedness that matters now, not speeding towards your target. Clock-time is gaining ground everywhere you look these days, even in Java, a market economy depends on it, but clock-time leads straight to the grave. You run out of it in a flash. Time exists objectively, of course it does, but we can inhabit it each in his or her own way. We can take up arms against it or work with it, but we don't have to just hurtle forwards into the bottomless pit.

Letting time pool is a random business—even the elderly simply have to be somewhere on time occasionally (for a colonoscopy, say, or a root-canal procedure—whatever it is, it's never pleasant) or get something done by Tuesday (which you can't quite put your finger on when Tuesday comes around). However, as you age, and one thing starts to inexorably follow another, a burst of non-sequential pooling is a boon. You can try flitting, for instance, from one puddle of time to another and then sitting in it as your fancy takes you, rather than simply because it's the next in a line of puddles.

One of the first things I noticed from the moment I landed back home was how driven everyone's movements seemed to be, how directed, how *linear*. The airport was abuzz with mostly black-clad people going somewhere. In Java, on the other hand, time had ballooned between the calls to prayer—not for everybody every day, but noticeably all the same, especially in the village. Nobody honked or screamed insults at other drivers in traffic-jams in Java. Why would you? What would be the point? It wasn't a race to the finish, after all, you weren't going anywhere. Even the rice-farmers around our village, always ploughing, tilling, planting and harvesting, seemed to be working to a different rhythm from ours, endlessly orbiting in time, not battling it. At home time rarely pools—even in airport departure lounges, it's almost universally given over to a purpose, it almost always looks funnelled: I see even the elderly reading, telephoning, buying sandwiches, doing face yoga—contriving somehow to make use of the minutes and hours. People at home appear to be moving along a narrow strip of time, headed for some finishing line—nothing too cosmic (at least at Melbourne airport), just dinner or Christmas, although the older you get, the more *final* phrases like 'finishing line' sound.

In less frantically individualistic societies than ours, where time is less one's own, it will always pool. In her splendidly accessible book on time, called just *Time*, the American writer Eva Hoffman, who was born in Poland, remarks on how struck she was when she arrived in North America as a teenage girl to find people hurrying to achieve something in their lives. Amazingly, Americans still believe they can arrive at a destination (apart from the local crematorium). In Poland, before the Wall came down, there was, as she puts it, 'really nothing much to hurry towards'. And so they *played*, as my table companion Hans might have put it—in particular, they played by talking. In Russia, before the Iron Curtain lifted, at least to some extent, I swam in the same kind of sea of unfunnelled time, even though I was still young. Some called it not a sea, but a bog (and still do). Whatever it was, it was no spa pool, but we did talk—deliciously and with gusto and some of us with panache.

There's a catch, however, to living in pools of playtime, even if you've well and truly paid off the mortgage. As Eva Hoffman emphasises, without time—and so without death, *pace* the gurus of the immortality industry—there is no sense in anything, no 'sanity'. Mortality, as she writes unflinchingly, is the prerequisite for meaning on this planet. To play is healthy, of course, but you must play within boundaries and by the clock, or else it's all just mucking about. A French friend of mine, Sophie Lambert, says the secret is to be simultaneously '*joueur et discipliné*' (playful and disciplined) in life. Since she's Gide's granddaughter, she has a gift for being precise and allusive at the same time. Life may be just a game, but it's certainly not just endlessly mucking about. It's game after game after game and then it stops.

For your life to make sense to you, what you do must have some consequence, so overall you must point forwards, even if you point in every direction on the compass at different times during your journey, just like a passenger on the Piccadilly Line. Otherwise it will become a swampy dreamscape, like the back-to-front world Alice finds herself in when she steps through the looking-glass. Who wants the retelling of their life to sound like some nonsense poem by Lewis Carroll where nothing is linked rationally to what comes next?

'Twas brillig, and the slithy toves
Did gyre and gimble in the wabe;
All mimsy were the borogoves,
And the mome raths outgrabe.

'Beware the Jabberwock, my son!
The jaws that bite, the claws that catch!
Beware the Jubjub bird, and shun
The frumious Bandersnatch!'

And so on and so on. When she comes to the end of 'Jabberwocky', Alice declares the poem 'very pretty', although she admits that 'it's rather hard to understand!'. To be blunt, she couldn't 'make it out at all', but was too coy to say so. At the end of a completely unsignposted life, any one of us might say that same thing. 'Somehow it seems to fill my head with ideas,' she muses, 'only I don't exactly know what they are! However, somebody killed something: that's clear, at any rate.' It's the sort of thing Rita might have said ten years ago after watching an episode of *Miss Marple*. Worryingly, it's the sort of thing I'm starting to say myself now after watching an episode of *Miss Marple*. Carroll's 'The Walrus and the Carpenter' is also sheer lunacy, but intelligible lunacy—no, oysters can't walk, but everyone knows what oysters and walking are. Lunacy is not quite so amusing in real life. In the corridors at St Ursula's it makes me weep.

Not all silly verse is nonsense verse, though: Edward Lear's 'The Owl and the Pussycat', for instance, makes perfect sense, despite the bong-tree, the runcible spoon, the money and honey wrapped up in a five-pound note, and all the other sillinesses. There are connections, there are consequences: the Owl and the Pussycat go sailing for a year and a day in search of a wedding ring, which they eventually find on the end of a pig's nose and buy for a shilling. They go on to be married by a turkey. Their time is spent purposefully, yet unhurriedly and pleasurably. Bliss. I'd go to sea with them, nobody wants a Jabberwock of a life. There may be no ultimate purpose to anything, but so what? There will be some point to each experience, even if it's only pleasure.

In short, for a well-lived life, and for a good old age in particular, as we circle the black hole of death, it's vital that each of us find his or her own ideal rhythm, balancing clock-time against some way of being-in-the-world that is more about being rooted than achieving anything. One thing will still come after another, obviously, even the pools of *yutori* we swim in, but our sense of consequence must first be prised away from our sense of achievement.

I can do the maths: I know time is getting short. Yet it's bizarre: the less time there is left, the less anxious I seem to feel about how I spend it! I meander more, I notice the colour of the sky with subtle pleasure, I snooze unhurriedly after lunch, I daydream a lot and pat the dog, I work with time as much as I can, not against it. If I miss the train, I wait contentedly for the next one. I have rambling conversations with friends, I take a zigzag route on my walks into town, I read what takes my fancy, I watch whatever I'm in the mood for on Netflix, I go to bed early and get up late. If I want to go to Java for a week or three, I do. I achieve very little, but my roots are deep and fat and full of sap.

Sugar and Spice

Another thing I noticed when I first stepped off the plane from Java (apart from how driven everyone looked, and the crowds of women wearing black—black slacks, black sweaters, black coats, black shoes, black everything) was the sex. The air was thick with sex—or at least the theatre of it. It hadn't been like that the previous day in Yogyakarta. Now everyone over twelve looked 'up for it': suave, sluttish, slinky, sullen, strapping, strutting, or just stretched out, snoozing—every last one of them, from the graceful to the greasy, was on parade! The cut of the clothes, the shoes, the hair, the stylishly trimmed chins, the brightly painted lips, the way they walked and looked around, alert, sharp-eyed, and reached over to touch their friends … at Sydney it was show time! 'Look at me,' they all seemed to be saying as they passed you on the concourse, 'look at me!' In French this provocative way of comporting yourself is called more precisely *'m'as-tu vu'* (Have you noticed me? Come on—take a look!) With your bare, bronzed legs, your hair an expensive just-out-of-bed (but whose?) *chef-d'oeuvre*, have I noticed you? Oh, yes, I've noticed you—we all have.

Actually, I rather like it. After Java it's confronting, but I like it. It's playful and mildly arousing. Java is so *modest* by comparison, desire there so understated and tightly choreographed that you can end up feeling the need for a bolt of something earthier. For a kick-start in Yogyakarta, for example, a bit of erotic effervescence, a touch of pepper or dash of spice, you'd have to try somewhere foreign—Nanamia Pizzeria, say, or the ViaVia café further up the street. I once watched Islamic pole-dancing at a fun-fair in Wonosobo, but it was fun for the whole family. There was wriggle but no sizzle. Yet the erotic can be vivifying, surely. Why live without it? It's on show wherever you look in Australia, there's no escaping it—from Nigella Lawson to the postman, everyone seems intent on looking beddable all the time—but at a certain point parading with any flair becomes a challenge. Wizened with sagging skin and rheumy eyes, we should probably stick to gawping from the sidelines. Or is there a middle way?

If the Roman poet Lucretius is to be believed, not just Sydney airport but the whole universe is 'a dance with Venus'—a sexual performance. 'Love' just provides some of the footwork for amicable copulation. Or something to that effect. In his day, of course, with high child mortality and a ripe old age far from assured, reproduction must have been at the top of everyone's list. Nowadays in the West average life expectancy is much longer than it was in Rome at the beginning of the first millennium—indeed, a quarter of the population where I live can hardly walk in a straight line without assistance, let alone cavort around Venus's dance floor—yet we are still fixated as a society on arousal and performance. What is the point of living on into old age in such a society? Why soldier on? Even if you could still dance, who would dance with you?

For older men, as everyone knows, having sex is like 'trying to shoot pool with a rope', as George Burns put it. He was very old indeed for half of the twentieth century, chain-smoked cigars, so knew what he was talking about. (He claimed fresh air made him throw up. He died aged one hundred.) So what else is there? Billing and cooing? Cuddling and holding hands? Older women often complain they are practically invisible in a society that only values youth, but at least they don't have George Burns's problem. Many attract ardent admirers. Ian Fleming was one of them, remarking that 'older women are best because they think they might be doing it for the last time'. A lot of men would be delighted to be doing it for the last time but can't do it at all—at least, not spontaneously.

Gay men have both George Burns's problem *and* fail to be noticed, unless they overact shamelessly to draw attention to themselves. People walk straight into them in the street, waiters leave them sitting unwaited-upon at tables, shop assistants look startled if they address them, looking around to see where the disembodied voice has come from. I can't tell you how many times I've had people push in front of me while I've been queuing at the post office, say, or Haigh's Chocolates, only to be told when I protest: 'Oh I'm so sorry, I didn't see you there!' On the upside, gay couples are frequently fairly realistic about how sexual the relationship with their life-partner will remain over the years. Aspects of the partnership or marriage apart from sex may well have been nurtured and strengthened early on.

Be that as it may, does it really matter if we're out of the sexual running, even in a society as sex-obsessed as ours? Kevin Costner said that sex and golf were the two things you could always enjoy without being good at them, but even he might discover there are minimum performance standards. If Lucretius was right and the universe is indeed a dance with Venus, yet dancing is out of the question, does it matter? If you want to grow old well, it's worth being clear-eyed on this question. Amongst my older friends, there are several schools of thought.

Some think the moment they retired from the fray was when life finally burst into flower in every colour of the rainbow. Take Andrea, for instance. We were having muffins and tea at the gallery one afternoon, as we do from time to time when I'm in town. She was in gauzy pinks and feathery greys, looking rather Bloomsbury—indeed, attractive. 'Someone I was reading the other day,' she said, '… who on Earth was it? … names won't come, will they, names evaporate … someone rather grand, as I remember … Anyway, she thinks that the best thing about being old is being released from the stranglehold of sex. She says at last she's her own woman!' We chortled.

'Is that the way you feel?' I asked. 'Not that I'd call you *old* …' A minefield, this topic.

'Pretty much, yes. Given a new lease on life. Don't you?'

'No,' I said, 'I don't feel strangled at all, and I'm older and more crumpled than you are.'

'You're only a *bit* older.'

'I find every second counts.' *Yutori* is a boon, but life is indeed like a roll of toilet-paper, as some wit has observed: the closer you get to the end, the faster it goes until, with a little wobble, nothing's left.

We'd actually started talking about Picasso and his female figures, not about sex as such, having just looked at his bare-breasted 'Woman with a Fan' in the exhibition upstairs. It roots you to the spot, that painting. Then we drifted on to another striking portrait we'd just looked at of a woman with her left breast bared by Félix Vallotton, one of the Nabis. Now in a thoroughly French mood, we recalled those riveting marble sculptures of naked grooms restraining their rearing horses in the Louvre, which brought to mind that astonishing painting, also in the Louvre, of Gabrielle d'Estrées, Henry IV's mistress, sitting up in a bath, naked to the waist, having her right nipple pinched by her naked sister, also sitting up in the bath. Conversations with Andrea always have a sort of higgledy-piggledy momentum. In a word, by the time the muffins and tea arrived, we were onto sex *tout court*. Lucretius would not have been surprised.

'Plato's on your side, of course,' I mumbled through my mouthful of blueberry muffin.

'What did he say?'

'I'll have to google it.'

'Google it, then.'

'He said,' I replied, mobile phone in hand: '"Old age has a great sense of calm and freedom; when the passions relax their hold, then … *blah blah blah* … we are free from the grasp of not just one mad master but of many."'

'I couldn't have put it better myself. The world opens up for you. You once were blind, and now can see. "Calm" is going a bit far, though.' That was true. I wouldn't like her calm. I like the way Andrea is always on the *qui vive*.

'And Sophocles said something pithy, too, along the same lines ... hang on, I'll google Sophocles as well. *S-o-p-h-o-c-l-e-s o-l-d a-g-e s-e-x*. Yes, here it is in Plato's *Republic*. Isn't it miraculous? Instant wisdom from 329 BC. "Oh be quiet, man," he says—one of his companions is asking him if he can still get it up with women. "Honestly, I'm pretty happy to have left all that behind. It's like I've finally made a getaway from some insane, sadistic taskmaster."' (*Mumble, mumble* as I quickly read on. Nobody wants *The Republic* word for word over tea and blueberry muffins.) 'The rest of them, the other "old birds of wrinkly feather" he's drinking with take the opposite view. When they were young they spent "every night carousing, partying, whoring and whatnot". I wonder what "whatnot" was, by the way. Any ideas? The poor fellows are in anguish, "thinking that what they've lost is what really matters, that they really lived back then and so now they might as well be dead".' I suspect half the male population still thinks this, keeping suicide at bay with golf, guns and a spot of gardening. It's hard to feel even manly, let alone hungry for life, if your penis won't stand up. It's crucial—a matter of life and death—to have more strings to your bow than carousing, partying, whoring and whatnot.

Andrea stole a chunk of my muffin and said: 'But you don't feel out of the running, I gather, even though ...' Even though I am an old bird of wrinkly feather, but Andrea forbore to spell it out.

'No, I feel as interested as I ever did, although less urgently so,' I said, 'and much less romantically. Lots of people my age do. Some women might hanker after a romance as well in their later years, but a lot of men, I suspect, just want to have a spot of fun now and again.' Gore Vidal said that he never missed an opportunity to have sex or go on television, but I had in mind a more sporadic interest, an itch to keep their hand in, if you know what I mean.

There are quite a few men whose appetites stay strong into their advanced old age. Sir Francis Younghusband, a British army officer who invaded Tibet disastrously in 1904 with twenty-nine trunks of clothes, fell head over heels in love in his late seventies, while still married, and stayed in love until he died (admittedly not too many years later). He was a close friend of Bertrand Russell's and a fierce opponent of buggery, although he was himself disarmingly partial to rogues who were 'profoundly spiritual' and more than smitten with the full-blooded mountaineer George Mallory. Everyone was, and in particular Lytton Strachey who wrote: 'George Mallory ... When that's been written, what more need be said? My hand trembles, my heart palpitates, my whole being swoons away at the words—oh heavens! heavens! ... he's six foot high, with the body of an athlete by Praxiteles, and a face—oh incredible ...' At the age of seventy-three Younghusband started an unusual new world religion which still functions (the World Congress of Faiths). Nevertheless, Sir Francis was an exception, a man of inexhaustible mental and physical resources. This Imperial hero of the North-West Frontier was never going to throw in the towel. A lot of men start throwing it in early middle age. The thing is to do whatever you want to do without anxiety.

Andrea had never heard of Sir Francis Younghusband or the World Congress of Faiths, but she knew perfectly well who André was. Gide did *precisely* what he wanted to do without anxiety. His appetite for sexual satisfaction may have eventually weakened, but even in his sixties it was easily excited. He went to Fez for the first time in 1932, for example, and 'gorged' himself on it for seven days until he was no longer 'thirsty'. When he got home from Morocco, he told the friend who had first suggested he might like it, Robert Levesque, that 'one ought to be able to go and spend three days there every couple of weeks to purge one's mind and body'. (In those days Fez was too far to go for a sexual escapade and nothing else. Nowadays it's just two hours from Cannes or Nîmes.) 'To purge one's mind and body' is a curious way to describe what you're aiming for in a bout of debauchery (of a kind, by the way, that most of us would now consider exploitative). Exactly what was purged from his mind *and body* is not explained here, but for Gide, sex—unbridled *volupté*—meant the release from some 'insane, sadistic taskmaster', not subjection to one. Which taskmaster was Gide escaping in Morocco? I suspect it was monotheism in all its manifestations. His sense of rapturous release in Fez reminds me, oddly enough, of the wave of ecstasy washing over the *kampung* in Java at Eid-al-Fitr when the sighting of the crescent moon signals the end of Ramadan and the breaking of the fast. The spirit and the body come joyfully back to life. After weeks or months or even years of fasting, an orgy—for some of us, both men and women—restores a balance. Quite simply, as Ogden Nash put it: 'Home is heaven and orgies are vile, but you need an orgy once in a while.' In Fez today sex is still offered until nightfall in the bustling cobbled laneways of the medina amongst all the mosques, the hammams, and the myriad shops and stalls, especially along Talaa Kebira up where the air smells of cedarwood, although not on the bland boulevards of the *nouvelle ville*. What's offered is usually touted as a *'massage berbère'*. To this day Moroccan men seem remarkably at ease about taking pleasure in sex with whomever they fancy, whatever the lawbooks might have to say about it.

Despite waning desire, almost twenty years after this trip to Fez, now eighty-one, Gide was contemplating yet another trip to Morocco, to Marrakech this time, to purge his mind and body again. The spirit was still astonishingly willing, but the flesh now really was weakening fast. Again, it was Robert Levesque who had whetted his appetite for erotic adventure. Levesque, now teaching at a *lycée* in Fez, wrote to Gide as winter set in to persuade him to come down to Morocco again, dangling first Tangier in front of him ('a quite indecent town', he called it enticingly) and then Marrakech.

'I still put Marrakech at the top of the list ...' Gide wrote. 'This is because, despite the fact that it's so easy to come by, sex there has kept its idyllic charm; you breathe it everywhere you go, you meet it at every step, no day is ever gloomy because every single moment is festooned with caresses ... Everyone is on the prowl, offering himself; in the torchlight, eyes and lips shine; everywhere you glimpse the outline of bodies coupling ...'

Just Gide's sort of thing, of course, but within weeks, before he could make the journey south, he sickened and died.

Not afraid of the ire of some peevish god, nor seeking to escape the cycle of rebirth, Gide was free to take pleasure in living out his fantasies of sexual intimacy until there was no Gide. We may deeply disapprove of how he did this, but the point I was making to Andrea was that some men take pleasure in sex until a very advanced age. Gide would have thought, as Diana Athill thought of her own affairs with married men, that in enjoying himself as he did he wasn't harming anyone at all.

Athill, who died not long ago at 101, is a particularly

articulate example of those many women who hanker after more than a nice night out now and again in the autumn of their lives. Two particular women friends of mine popped into my head, both love-struck anew at seventy-five, writing daily love letters to their beloveds—their loves, their *inamorati*, their objects of desire. 'Lovers' seems too colourless a word for the swains (both married men, although not, I gather, on active duty) who have brought them alive in a surge of passion when all seemed lost. My friend Barbara's mother Nancy was still enjoying a busy love-life when she was well into her nineties: one Saturday afternoon in recent memory she was still pushing one gentleman caller out of the laundry window at the back of the house as the next one started jiggling his key in the door at the front. All the same, Andrea's sense of a burgeoning new life as their sexual obligations fall away strikes me as common.

The fly in the ointment for those of us, men or women, who *are* still open to amorous entanglements is that, while you may desire a whole slew of others (the gangly, let's say, or the brown, the angelic, the sporty or anyone Egyptian), few are likely ever again to desire you. Virtually nobody at all on the face of the planet will desire you in the way you dream of, whatever the internet-dating sites might promise. Why would anyone desire you like that? Lovable—yes, desirable—not really. You can forget the *Kama Sutra*, you can put the Crow Position and the Position of a Herd of Cows right out of your mind, and concentrate on less athletic forms of intimacy and affection. (By the same token, to be scrupulously honest, a quick read-through of the Indian classic, especially if your copy is lushly illustrated, as mine is, can sharpen the memory deliciously, leading at the very least to more adventurous biting, kissing, pressing and scratching with the nails, if that's your thing. Hitting is also possible.) I am intrigued, might I add, since the subject has come up, by the way Hindus seem not to object to carnal pleasure *as such*—indeed, it's a duty to indulge the passions, according to the Hindus, so long as you carry out your other duties (to your family, for instance, and to freeing yourself from rebirth—eventually, that is, there's no great hurry). Women's duties seem more burdensome than men's. Lasciviousness seems not to be a sin *as such*, however. In fact, sin seems not to be a Hindu concept at all. It is the Middle Eastern deity ('I am the LORD and there is no other') who jealously threatens violence like an abusive father if we love as we wish and not as he has commanded.

'But these sites,' said Andrea, catching my drift, but ignoring India, 'for mature …'

'… players. Yes. And their admirers. A pig in a poke, as a rule,' I said, 'although you never know. Have you ever given it a go? It depends what kind of love you're looking for, of course. No strings attached, long-term monogamous, taste it and see …' I cast an eye around at the dozen or so ageing customers in the art gallery café. On a weekday afternoon, nobody there was under sixty, although on the whole it was a sprightly, smartly-dressed crowd. Nobody looked to be on the prowl, though. Fizzier than the ViaVia café in Yogyakarta, but any fizzing that *was* going on was very low-key.

'What I love now, I think, is dalliance,' I said after a pause, as a young man labelled CESAR briskly cleared the table. Cesar was very well-presented. 'Thank you, Cesar,' I said.

'No problem, sir,' he murmured. Was he Colombian?

'What *is* dalliance exactly?' Andrea asked, oblivious of Cesar. 'Isn't it just a posh word for having an affair?'

'Oh, no, it's got nothing to do with having an affair.

An affair is serious and quite often a betrayal, while a dalliance is a game, it's never a great love. It may even be chaste. There are rules, of course—times, places, moves.' The ViaVia every Saturday night from six to eight, for instance, upstairs. 'At its best, at its most skilfully and dangerously pursued, I really believe a dalliance is more delicious, more exciting, more … oh I don't know … rejuvenating than anything else on Earth. And you can dally almost anywhere, too—at the back of a bus or on national television—I've seen Stephen Fry do it on *QI* with the whole world watching.'

'Is *that* what that's called …' said Andrea.

'Perhaps that was more coquetry, now I come to think about it. Take Lord Krishna, then—blue-skinned Krishna, the god who sported with all those milkmaids, sixteen thousand of them. Flirted, dallied. I've got him up on my living-room wall at home—do you remember? With six maids, too, and twenty-six cows.'

'Of course I remember. Gouache on linen. The blue, that blue, that royal blue skin of Krishna's, almost midnight.'

'The thing is, every single one of those milkmaids

has already transcended the flesh. They're dancing with a god, they're dallying. It's erotic, but not sexual.'

'Heavenly. So it's a sort of middle way for you between passion and nothing at all.'

'A third way, let's say, rather than a middle one.'

'The young don't dally at all these days, do they.'

'They hardly need to. They copulate for a bit and then start a long-term relationship. They don't last, as we know, these LTRs—I mean the floods of dopamines to the brain and the dilated pupils—but they last long enough to enlarge the gene pool, so Venus is happy. Dallying comes later, I think. Don't you really ever dally nowadays, Andrea? Not at the behest of any taskmaster, obviously, but just for the life-enhancing fun of it?'

'Oh, not seriously, no.'

'Dallying doesn't have to be serious.'

Andrea thought for a moment, then asked: 'Do you know Diana Athill? You must know Diana Athill … lovely writer, literary editor at André Deutsch.'

'Yes, I do, as it happens, I was just thinking about her.' Athill gave up on romantic love in her forties, but *loved* for sixty more years, in many cases, as I've said other women's husbands—harmlessly, as far as one can tell. She had a penchant for black men.

The spirit was still willing, Diana Athill wrote about sex in her eighties or thereabouts, but the flesh was weak. Her boyfriend at the time—Sam, who was Caribbean—felt much the same way: sex was a lovely idea, he agreed, but the body does indeed eventually go against it. She said that being forced to fake what had been such an important pleasure in her life was more depressing than doing without sex altogether. She was, of course, a woman with a voluminous inner life.

'Well, the marvellous thing about life beyond sex for Diana Athill,' Andrea went on, 'is that you have so much time for other things—for thinking about other things as well as doing them. And do you remember my friend Greta? Greta loves sex, but even Greta—who has a fabulous new boyfriend, by the way, reminds you of whatshisname, Clive Owen, but with class—even Greta says that sex three times a day is fine for a day or two, but then you really want to get on with other things. I know exactly what she means—not that I've ever, you know ... I actually find that, as sex ebbs, the wider world gets more and more fascinating. Even dallying must take up time you could be spending on more interesting things.'

'Like what?' It was a serious question. *What?* Not quilting or taking classes in Chinese, presumably.

'This, for example—sitting here with an old friend. A thousand other things—when sex stops hogging the limelight. With sex out of the way, you can let little things in your life grow into big things and a couple of big things shrink till they're little. I've gone back to the piano again, I've taken up bonsai, I read whatever I want whenever I want, I don't try to keep up, I fly up to Madang whenever I feel like it ...'

'Madang, yes,' I murmured. I had vivid memories of Madang.

'Obviously you can learn the piano and have sex at the same time—in fact, the piano is perfect for setting the mood, the flute will get you nowhere—but disentangled from sex, all sorts of things that were stunted grow up tall and strong and put out shoots.' She was waving one hand around in a way I liked. A delicate silver bracelet on her wrist flashed in the light. 'But friendship, I think, in my case, is what I enjoy having more time for now, above all for my old friends—people

I just love.' I nodded. That was precisely it. *Friendship*. The love that can never be bought. You had to be worth making friends with in the first place, that was a given, but Andrea was. You ventured into her inner world at your peril, but once safely inside you could revel in its abundance. In our times, it's our friendships—affections, attachments, understandings and intimacies, some long-lasting, some momentary—that knit us together, fashioning our very selves for us, making each one of us utterly distinct. What a vast patchwork of colours, shapes and sizes these friendships form! Once upon a time in Europe it was probably more the way it still is in Java: it was your family, your religion, your 'people' (your *suku*) who made you so singularly you.

When the celebrated astronomer and astrophysicist Carl Sagan wrote that for infinitesimally small creatures such as we are, the vastness of the universe is bearable 'only through love', I can imagine he had in mind not just a mother's for her child or a married couple's for each other but a kaleidoscopic panoply of possible loves—passionate, pitying, playful (some friends are simply play-friends, a bit of a lark), and also amorous, tender, ethereal, muscular, mystical, animal, blissful, businesslike, blindly jealous or just blind, a virtually boundless web of intensely felt, vivifying attachments. Chillingly (since love is so fragile, so quick to dry up or disappear, leaving an infinite emptiness behind), I think Sagan was right, which is why the night sky is terrifying to the point of ecstasy sometimes. And of all these loves I think friendship is the most difficult and most rewarding kind. Souls you love as your own soul. There won't be many of these souls—a handful will do—but each will be as big as the moon. (Not that we believe in souls.) Yes, affairs or even just being dizzy with desire, like one of Krishna's milkmaids, can blind you to a whole array of other kinds, less sensual kinds, of intimacy.

We sat happily for a while in a bright shaft of afternoon sunlight, slowly draining another pot of tea and silently considering the intimate relationships that had nourished us over the years, along with one or two that had not nourished us at all. Bit by bit, as the decades tick over (and in this Andrea was quite right), it is intimacy with all its different plotlines, in all its different hues, that sustains us more and more, not passion, which, in her words, can start to look distinctly 'silly' at a certain age—untimely and therefore comic.

For all that, generally speaking, in our society these days it's the kind of love that marriage celebrates that is our highest goal in life. Even some homosexuals see marriage (of all things) as the supreme good. Love is not enough, it appears, nor friendship, in their boundless variety: love must also be hopeful of monogamy and publicly solemnised if it is to be prized above all else. Many males live out their entire lives without any friends at all, just a spouse. Indeed, I doubt my own father, for all his affability and warm-heartedness, had any friends—companions at the bowls club latterly, but nobody I'd call a friend, no one he loved intensely simply because they were who they were and he was who he was (if I might resort to Montaigne's arresting description of his friendship for Étienne de La Boétie). Yet, until the modern era, if historians such as A.C. Grayling are to be believed, it was friendship in its many forms that was humanity's highest goal—apart from a love for God, of course, which for the deeply devout made friendship dicey. Marriage underpinned the social structure, obviously, and love for one's spouse, if it blossomed, made the arrangement much more pleasurable, but it was friendship that gave life its charge, its zest, its exhilaration and its lasting joy. No doubt the modern appreciation of women as distinct beings—beings with an inside to their lives as well as an outside—has enhanced the attractiveness of marriage. As recently as the early eighteenth century Alexander Pope opined that 'most women have no characters at all'. For 'character' men turned to their friends.

There is also the question of one's Great Love, the man or woman who is neither simply a friend nor a spouse, or even a friend or a spouse, but somebody and something else entirely, something for which we scarcely have the words. Katharina calls it 'the hearth love' in your life. This Great Love (and I've had two over a lifetime, one at a time) may be your pivot, anchor or keystone, loved as you love yourself, may be all the things a god is supposed to be (not Jesus, obviously, lest I be misunderstood, but a god), yet not everything, of course. Whatever that song may say (I can hear them crooning it in my head), *No, you are not my everything.*

'I do like to have a beautiful enemy there, too, somewhere amongst my friends, I must say.' I was partly talking to myself, just to air the notion, which had fascinated me for years, ever since I'd come across it in one of Emerson's essays (or, to be honest, in an article about it). 'It's the excitement of making mine what isn't mine at all. Taming him. Or (thrillingly) being tamed. I like friends who are ruby-hard. Friendships like wine or honey are all very well, but the glowing, ruby-hard ones are best.' Before Andrea (who is more an opal than a ruby) could say anything about beautiful enemies, I added: 'And sometimes I like an unequal friendship, do you know what I mean? I like to grow close to someone …' But words began to fail me. I paused and blinked. 'Not every amour in life, surely, needs to have its roots in a vast, symphonic coming together of minds, souls and bodies.' I gestured wildly to demonstrate how vast these symphonies could sometimes be. 'Now and again I like to be intimate with someone who has no interest at all in all those things of the mind I've spent my life immersed in, spent it *brandishing*, really, someone I have nothing in common with but feelings. Just feelings of tender regard. There's an inner life, but made of different stuff from mine.' I could see Andrea was on the alert for humbug.

'A *scherzo*—I see. But what do you talk about?'

'We don't talk much.'

'I find it hard to imagine you not talking.'

But I really don't. I just rest in the affection of someone who thinks—I don't know for what concatenation of strange reasons, who can ever know?—that I am in some real sense 'beautiful'. In other words, I sometimes take my repose in someone who sees past my words to what I am and wants me for that—wants to be kind to me. Especially in the torrid zones, where (rousingly) I feel I'm behind enemy lines every second of every day, surrounded by adversaries I might call a truce with, just for the afternoon, and rest in. Who knows? Who will tame whom?

Apropos of things equatorial, Cesar, looking very pre-Columbian in the harsh sunshine, tamed only by his starched white shirt, nodded inscrutably as we made our way past him to the escalator. Cesar doubtless had little interest in Dostoyevsky or Hindu metaphysics. When it comes to waiters, though, you just never know these days. He could easily have had a PhD in astrophysics.

Outside on the street, as the sun dipped behind the

skyscrapers across the park, Andrea and I said goodbye at the bus stop, she almost wraithlike in her faded pinks and greys at that time of day—a tenderly mortal moment, as leave-takings always are at a certain age, even when you're as fit as a fiddle and it's just the bus to Birchgrove. Off she sailed into the dusk, which was heavy with the smell of squashed figs. What could be headier? Dusk is a delicious time, even in colder climates, a sensual time, a time of suddenly sharpened appetites. When evening falls, as the American writer James Salter once worded it in a piece he wrote for that journal of sharpened appetites, *GQ*, 'there is the call of the boulevards'. That was some thirty years ago—I doubt many dally or loiter or prowl on actual boulevards any more, they just go shopping, except in Paris—but it's a graphic trope. Needless to say, in Paris boulevards are real boulevards, and you can saunter on them any evening you choose, alive in the half-light with unquenched longings, open to adventure and enchantment. It's an eventless pastime for the elderly, but still a pleasure. 'Haunting the boulevards' and 'baths' (*piscines*), for instance, was something he did for years, usually with a companion, whenever he was in Paris without his wife—at least until his appetites became less urgent (as they eventually always do). Salter had lived in Paris, naturally, and, as it happens, one of his favourite writers was none other than André Gide. There is in Salter, I think, more than a touch of Gide's high-minded sensuality—high-minded in the retelling of it, that is.

Making my way through the dark to my hotel that evening, the city a waterfall of lights against the blue-black velvet of the sky, I reflected on how faint the 'call of the boulevards' was, or at least how infrequent it had become, whereas the call of an early night in bed with a good book was more and more often irresistible. It beckoned as a delicious spot of *yutori* to buffer the coming day. As the city came out to play—as lights came on and bands struck up and thousands, even hundreds of thousands, of players and spectators dressed and coiffed to catch the eye milled in the streets and bars, excited—I headed back for some 'fruitful monotony', if I might borrow Bertrand Russell's brilliant term for one of happiness's vital ingredients. I would first order room service and then fructify at my leisure.

All the same, having been to Marrakech and Fez

many times, if more innocently than Gide, I like to keep the idea of such places handy, just to keep my spirits up if they need raising, *faute de mieux.*

Mellow Fruitfulness

Bertrand Russell had a point. Alone in my featureless room that evening, all I did was lie on the bed and stare at the off-white walls, the fawn carpet and the fresh, mustardy curtains, not even attempting to read in any serious fashion, just dipping in and out of something Irish I had little appetite for. It's astonishing how boring modern hotel rooms can be. In my hotel in Java, by way of contrast, none of the rooms had been boring, being the living-rooms and bedrooms of old village houses snoozing amongst the vines, the palms and the pools of froggy water. There the rooms had been blue and green and orange, with terraces and bathrooms half-open to the sky—rooms with their roots in village lives, rooms that were new and at the same time ancient. However, this budget room of mine high up in a faceless tower near Central Station was numbingly boring, beigely, banally, bog-standard boring. And yet, curiously, in the blankness something stirred, as Russell suggested it might. It is precisely from nothing that the biggest ideas sometimes spring, after all—the universe, for example. It was because He was bored with the boredom of infinite nothingness, according to Alberto Moravia in *La Noia*, that God started playing around with Chaos and created the universe—the sky, the seas, Adam and Eve and so on. In the beginning was boredom and now look at what we've got. The Vatican put *La Noia* on its index of prohibited books immediately.

What exactly stirred in me is hard to say. I didn't create a universe, lying there on my bed, but once I started to practise simply being present, as Russell would have had me do, I did indeed feel happily fruitful, at least intermittently. Quite juicily, as a matter of fact, at times, even lushly. In small doses, stillness can startle you sometimes by bubbling over with wild couplings— this thought with that, these images with those, these memories tumbling about helter-skelter in your head with fantasies about what might have been. I scurried about after memories like a child chasing butterflies: to no practical purpose.

I thought first about Cesar's nose, because big, hooked noses happen to rivet me, and then (pell-mell) about Colombia, Peru, Pizarro, the Inca, my mind buzzing like a beehive while my body lay quite still, and then I thought about Tahiti and the Gauguins I'd seen that afternoon, spiralling down eventually to alight on Andrea (pink and grey) and all the things she now had time for, freed as she was from the yoke of sex: piano lessons, books, and some very wild shores indeed. (Madang, for instance, my mind looped over to Madang, where I'd spent a sultry week a lifetime ago, and to Miklouho-Maclay—the Russian explorer—and to St Petersburg where he died.) And friendship, naturally, above all I dwelt on friendship. After an eventful life, Andrea was now 'cultivating her garden', like Voltaire's Candide (but for different reasons), growing just those plants that really nourished and pleased her, freed from the choking briars of sexual feelings. The plant that flourished most robustly in her garden was friendship. And she was content.

Yet (I thought to myself) there was a more deeply

rooted reason for her happiness, surely: she was creative. Her garden was not just nourishing, with its sexual entanglements now weeded out, it was also a work of art.

God only knows, for all our leisure it's not easy to be creative, yet to live well right to the end without being creative is virtually impossible. The painter Kartika Affandi (one of Indonesia's most celebrated artists today) put it like this to me, gaily, one day over lunch on her verandah, out in the picturesque, absurdly green middle of nowhere north of Yogyakarta: 'If you have no creativity in your life, then you will just live from day to day.' Can that be true? What did Kartika mean by 'creativity'? Can anyone at all be creative? Kartika was herself the daughter of a renowned artist, Affandi, perhaps Indonesia's most highly acclaimed painter, so Kartika had a head start.

Kartika does not live 'from day to day'—you can see that as soon as she comes out onto the verandah to greet you, although how she does live is at first a mystery. She is what might be called 'young and antique'—that's how the hero of Fellini's *8½* describes his muse (played by a radiant Claudia Cardinale). Ancient and wrinkled, in every gesture and word Kartika is yet as lively as a child, a bit of a tomboy (weirdly), an eighty-four-year-old tomboy, full of mischief, meaning to live, she said, to 117. She's Buddhist by choice in that Muslim heartland, and so bare-headed, quickly intimate, the mother of eight, and the first woman to file for divorce in the Republic of Indonesia. She paints prolifically, turbulently, harshly, rarely sweetly, as only men have painted in Indonesia as a rule. She excels at self-portraits in particular, some of them shockingly explicit in sexual terms, even depicting her own nakedness, cocking a snook at the traditional Javanese notion of female modesty, decency and refinement. 'I strike my own gong, you see,' she said, beaming at me over the nasi goreng, 'which is against the rules here.'

'What's wrong with living from day to day?' I ventured.

'Because same same same same every day,' she said. 'Like a lizard. Why even bother? For artists every day is out of the ordinary, extraordinary, *luar biasa*, unfamiliar, because art breaks up the world and puts it back together again in a way never seen before. Each poem, each painting.' Which is, as we know, what God did with Chaos. (I'm writing this from hasty notes, by the way—her English is good but eccentric, my Indonesian poor. But I think I caught the thrust of what she said.)

Kartika Affandi, although not from the nobility, has no master, living a bit like one of those minor Russian aristocrats (at least from my perspective), like Turgenev, say, on his estate of Spasskoye, or Chekhov in his modest country house at Melikhovo outside Moscow. Actually, Chekhov wasn't a member of the nobility any more than Kartika is. All the same, at Melikhovo in particular, with its small pond, abundant garden and handful of servants, the estate where Chekhov wrote his plays and had friends to stay and endlessly talk, life must often have been much as it is now at Kartika's house at the foot of Mt Merapi, a place where people constantly come and go, set in a lush garden with a pond, a place where it doesn't feel as if life is ever lived 'from day to day' as a chain of gratuitous incidents, or as an endless series of repetitions, either (although everyone has to get up, eat and clean their teeth every day), but more as a series of astounding discoveries or illuminations, where the outer and the inner are ceaselessly in conversation. To listen to Kartika is to find yourself watching the slow dance of what is clearly seen with what is deeply felt. In a word—art. Kartika's house and garden are the perfect combination of monotony and fruitfulness.

The slow dance. If you want to stay creative as you grow older, it's not simply a matter of deciding to write your memoirs, say, when time permits, or taking up photography or redesigning your back garden to make it Zen. To do those things creatively, making patterns with words, light and stones where there had been none, you must first spend time with your own feelings, trying to imagine others' feelings, and take pleasure in what happens when the outer and inner worlds begin to play with each other. If you have no inner life you're unlikely to be curious about what happens when these two worlds collide (about art, in other words), and you will certainly not be curious about what it feels like to be someone else. John Cleese, in a clever, funny talk he gave on creativity years ago, said you also need a sense of humour if you want to be creative. You can't manufacture a sense of humour, but if you don't have one, then you might indeed be better off reporting facts. Art is not about reporting. Indeed, if Edward Said and Theodor Adorno are to be believed, the nearer you are to your end, the less your creativity is likely to refer directly to the outer world at all.

Bob Dylan, whether or not you think he deserved his Nobel Prize for Literature, has led a dauntingly creative life since he began playing in bands in high school in Minnesota over sixty years ago. He's been playing, singing and composing ever since: a dazzling musical range from folk songs, American standards, political and gospel to hard rock. After converting to born-again Christianity in his thirties to widespread derision, he even wrote some remarkably fine gospel songs such as 'Slow Train Coming' and 'Every Grain of Sand'. He was 'sunshiny' (to quote the *Guardian*) for three short years. Still, as he himself pointed out, even Jesus only preached for three years. With less lustre, Dylan has written poetry, a novel, a volume of memoirs, and even painted, quite successfully. This explosion of creativity in one man is impressive. Another American singer-songwriter, with a face as haunting as Dylan's, Jeff Buckley, captured the essence of Dylan's creative power when he called him darkly romantic in the manner of Leonard Cohen and Patti Smith, having in mind, he said, 'a sensibility that sees everything, and has to express everything, and still doesn't know what the fuck it is, it hurts that bad'. In other words, you see, you feel, you hurt, you create. 'It just madly tries to speak whatever it feels,' Buckley went on, 'and that can mean vast things. That sort of mentality can turn a sun-kissed orange into a flaming meteorite, and make it sound like that in a song.' It's a sensibility few have. More commonly oranges remain oranges. Only gods and fairies can zap an orange with a finger or wand and turn it instantly—*whoosh!*—into a ball of fire.

I mention Dylan, to be frank, because I was struck by his response to people who talk about finding themselves. 'But life isn't about finding yourself or finding anything,' Dylan said, 'it's about creating yourself.' That's it in a nutshell, really. Along the way, you might write *Othello* or compose 'Romeo and Juliet'. I was surprised to hear Dylan say this—I'd have expected something more Mr. Tambourine Man from him, I suppose, a few allusions to 'magic swirlin' ships' and 'dancin' spells'. Mind you, dancin' spells are also a fine idea.

Buried deep inside the madness Buckley mentions, the hurt of 'not knowing what the fuck it is' you see and feel when you're on the verge of creating something worthwhile, lies the hurt of not knowing whether the fuck your art is redemptive of your inner nothingness or just an expression of it. Astonishingly, in *8½* Federico Fellini does both: in making a film about a man who has 'nothing to say' in a barren world where 'there's nothing at all anywhere', Fellini ends up making a film 'with everything in it', ending with a 'flash of joy and love' and an explosion of creative energy. For most of us there is no remedy for the hurt Buckley alludes to, it will go on forever. The German artist Anselm Kiefer found an illuminating, fortifying middle way: 'Life is an illusion,' he said. 'I am held together in the nothingness by art.' It won't suit everyone, but it repays contemplation. It was an insight akin to Kiefer's that took my breath away, quickened me, jolted me awake, in the nDalem Pujokusuman pavilion in Yogyakarta, watching some children learning to dance. The children were weaving selves in the emptiness out of Indian myth and classical tradition. Their art would hold them together—of course, being Muslims, they probably would not think of life in the world as mere illusion, as the Hindu creators of the form once did. All the same, with their mobile phones rarely out of their hands, many are indeed beginning to see life as meaningless tumult (*keributan yang tak berarti*), or so they tell me, and that is much the same thing. Art creates an oasis in which, briefly but often, the tumult is patterned and meaning appears. (So does religion, needless to say. Indeed, from the point of view of some heretical Muslim saints, that's all religion ever is: garments clothing non-being, words filling emptiness. However, the children I saw learning to dance in the nDalem Pujokusuman pavilion in Yogyakarta are unlikely to have ever heard of these saints. These days their views are too shocking to be spoken of.)

Until, that is, the finishing line finally comes into view. One good thing about creating when we're nearing the end is that we're more likely to thumb our noses at authority and just create as we wish. *Seventy … and to hell with it* is the telling name of bestselling Indian writer Shobhaa Dé's latest memoir. We don't care when we take up our pen or brush if what we produce is second-rate or misunderstood—we're *hors de combat* now. We do what we do for the sheer kid-again pleasure of doing it—and to hell with it. We write our poems, we weave and pot and learn Italian for the pure fun of it *as we do it*. We have no future. From where I stand, it's the young who seem more likely to respect the current pieties than the ageing are, one blinkered eye firmly on what is fashionable here and the other one on what is *de rigueur* in New York. Or Berlin or Paris. (Not in Cairo or Calcutta, obviously.)

We all know there is a finishing line, having often turned it into art, sometimes with a certain brio, from a safe distance. Novels, poems and plays have been written about death, corpses and deathbed scenes have been painted in manifold poses, both heroic and domestic, countless sonatas, quartets and symphonies with death and dying at their heart have been composed—Beethoven, Schubert, Stravinsky, Bartók, Richard Strauss, any composer you can think of, really (even Elton John had a go, lamenting the death of Marilyn Monroe). But when the end of the line eventually appears out of the fog right in front of us, when we can reach out and touch it, and peer into the nothingness beyond, we may create differently. If there *is* anything there, nobody has ever seen it.

This brings me—or brought me, rather, lying on the bed in my beige and fawn eyrie that evening, listening to the hotel plumbing—to the question of Late Style, a term made memorable by Edward Said. Style should not be too late, that goes without saying, gaga never being good, although Shostokovich's melancholy final string quartet (No. 15 in E-flat minor) for example, with its first movement to be played, he instructed, 'so that flies drop dead in mid-air', was very late indeed, largely composed on his death-bed in a Moscow hospital. What gives the quartet its transcendent force is precisely the macabre dance around the question of whether or not utter nullity can be redeemed or only given vent to. Gide's rambling *So Be It* could hardly have been 'later', either, since he was dead within days of laying down his pen. 'I have made up my mind to write at random,' he begins, '[and] if I feel like contradicting myself, I shall contradict myself without hesitation. I shall not strive for "coherence". But shall not affect incoherence, either.' Both Shostakovich and Gide, each brilliantly inventive, exhibit signs of Said's Late Style syndrome, which he elaborated in talks he gave and his book *On Late Style* on the basis of Beethoven's last sonatas and quartets.

Can Said's Late Style ideas be distilled? In Beethoven, for example, Said saw a shift to focusing on structure, rather than melody; on a fragmentation and a loss of interest in continuity; on an irascible opposition to established conventions; on inwardness, rather than history. In other words, it's the Beethoven of the *Diabelli Variations*, not the *Eroica* Said was homing in on. Said's description of Late Style, however, sounds alarmingly like the modernist maxim that Simon Schama took such vigorous exception to in his *Civilisations* television series: that anything can be art if it's presented as art, no matter how disconnected from history. For Schama it's a sense of connectedness and continuity in art that gives it a vital spark. Even more alarmingly, it sounds like a conversation with Rita. Said's Late Style sounds startlingly like dementia. Indeed, one commentator on Late Style (Barbara Herrnstein Smith) has called it the 'senile sublime'. It is indeed arguably senile, but often far from sublime.

Is Late Style in Edward Said's sense a common response amongst artists to finding themselves at last, after all these years, on the edge of the actual abyss, staring into nothingness? It might fit well with Beethoven, for instance, who is the focus of Said's attention, or even Shakespeare, but the examples of artists who had no Late Style are innumerable. Tolstoy, for instance, looked within himself in old age and out of the blue found somethingness, not nothingness at all, so his Late Style was driven, coherent and redemptive. Nikolai Gogol also converted to Christianity, but failed to write anything redemptive. Part I of his phantasmagorical masterpiece *Dead Souls* illustrates precisely Said's conceit: it is unfinished, it is a series of variations on a simple 'folk melody' (the moral emptiness of serfdom), each one exquisitely detailed, and at its heart is a large blank: the scheming moral blank, empty and round like a zero with legs, Pavel Ivanovich Chichikov. However, Gogol died ten years after Part I of *Dead Souls* came out, not shortly afterwards. Writing about the carnival of nothingness had come naturally to him, as it does to many writers, but there's nothing natural about redemption in the twenty-first century, as there may have been in Dante's day. Now redemption is miraculous. Eventually Gogol burnt all his attempts to write a *Purgatory* or *Paradiso* to absolve him of the sin of having written such a rollicking *Inferno*.

What first sprang into my mind in this regard that evening in my beige room, however, was neither Tolstoy nor Gogol, but the recent Sherlock Holmes series from the BBC, with Benedict Cumberbatch inimitable in the leading role: *Sherlock* is a Late Style version of Conan Doyle and the cogent earlier versions. It's not for a moment about who done what why to whom, it's about the presentation of superbly acted (directed, lit, assembled) fragments, inventively reconfiguring the emptiness of the characters' lives—turning it outwards (to paraphrase Said). It's a sickening emptiness, it's a stylish spectacle. The joy of it is totally in the form. While the many writers and creators of *Sherlock* are not yet teetering on the edge of the abyss, the culture we all grew up in is. It's the culture that's Late, I think, and nearing its death. Art as an amusing assemblage of objects or pictures or sounds or words on the page, signifying very little, is in its heyday. So much of what we read, see and hear is unnervingly close to simply giving vent to nothingness, like the music of Philip Glass.

By the same token, the redemption of nothingness in art is also alive and well, although unlikely to grow out of religious belief these days. It springs instead from all the things Said believes Late Style commonly lacks: cohesiveness, connectedness and an engagement with history. The bridge most of us throw across the abyss of meaninglessness is good, old-fashioned, causally connected storytelling. Apparently we're hard-wired for it: whenever something happens in a story, especially a dramatic reversal of fortune, there is apparently a surge in neural activity in the brain. We come alive. And so we totter on into the fog, putting our faith in the frail structure of story until we can step back onto *terra firma* again—the solid ground of dailiness. Things still make no sense, but at least we've made it. For now. And so from childhood, in our hundreds of millions, we read novels about eventful lives, watch movies about eventful lives, and gorge ourselves on sitcoms and crime series about chains of events—any sort of event: love affairs, marriages, murders, skulduggery, but especially adultery and murder, with hope at the end, pleasurably papering over the utter pointlessness of absolutely everything as prayer once did.

Strange to relate, I've gone off story. As a writer, I've spun plenty of stories in my time—about meeting my birth mother for the first time in middle age; about dealing within a framework borrowed from Dante with the hell of an HIV diagnosis in an era when the disease was terminal; about Turgenev's all-consuming love for a French opera singer; about Gide's double life in France and North Africa, to name but four—but increasingly I find myself more at home in gossiping about the human heart, darting out into the world and back inside again to write about what I have just seen—rock art in Cape York, a Laotian phrase book, Vladivostok, noses, friendship, dilettantism, leisure and the art of doing nothing—a thousand disparate things. I write essays and reflections, not narratives. Having reached my end days, why would I? Even when I decided to write about the experience of having a heart attack on a city street far from home, I wrote it as a collection of reflections on what days are for. Sorties these days, rather than stories. And then I come home. I have to sketch in a thread of some kind, of course, to guide my reader home with me, but it's not of the essence any more, as it is in a real storyteller. The essence is discovering what home is.

Of course, you have to leave home in the first place, as Cavafy reminds us (and Said reminds us by quoting the Greek poet), if you are to make your way back home enriched. Famously, in the poem 'The City', one Alexandrian (presumably) tells his friend, another Alexandrian, who is 'mouldering away' in the 'black ruins' of his day-after-day life in Egypt:

> You won't find a new country, won't find another shore.
> This city will always pursue you.
> You'll walk the same streets, grow old in the same neighbourhoods, turn grey in these same houses
> You'll always end up in this city. Don't hope for things elsewhere: there's no ship for you, there's no road.
> Now that you've wasted your life here, in this small corner, you've destroyed it everywhere in the world.

Start early if you want to visit 'harbours hitherto unseen', as he writes in another masterpiece, 'Ithaca', and sail home slowly with a cargo of 'nacre and coral, amber and ebony', with new knowledge as well, of course, with learning and understanding.

That said, as I strive to stay inventive, many things stay the same. The voice is the same, the deepest concerns unaltered: how to live well—*avoir une belle vie*—despite mortality, despite *everything*. On reflection, I think my Late Style is more visible in how I live than in how I write: as I age, and the years begin not just to fly but to hurtle by, I notice that the garden of my mind is much less French than it used to be, less geometric, less binary or symmetrical, less concerned about the impression it might make. There was always a secret door in the garden wall to allow for forays into balmier, headier, untidier corners where date palms grew, hibiscus rioted and jasmine trailed abundantly across the warm stone walls, but the main garden my mind used to take pleasure in was ordered and coherent. Over the years the secret door has sagged and hung open, the garden wall itself has begun to crumble, and everywhere you look it's a jumble of colours and shapes to delight the inner eye. The paths through it meander, instead of forming tight patterns, the fragrances are spicier, redolent of Gujarat or Java as often as not; it's a mishmash, it's unfinished, it adds up to nothing at all, *and I don't care*. Who'd have thought? Once upon a time I only went adventuring in that swathe of lands between Lisbon in the west and Greece in the east, with just a flying visit or two to the sweatier, sandier places further east towards Oman or along the coast of North Africa, places where the muezzins call believers to prayer five times a day and the alleyways smell of cigarettes and agarwood—as well as of garbage, of course, it's a pungent mix. My old stamping ground was deeply civilised and pretty in places, but not rapturously sensual, as my mind's garden now is. At my age there's really no downside to the rapturously sensual—none that I can think of, at least. A disciplined life with lots of playtime—that's my ideal—but well to the east of Suez these days. Ganesha rather than Diderot or Dante. The small, bronze dancing Ganesha on my windowsill back home again springs into my mind—one plump knee raised, his four arms held out at graceful angles, oiled, curled hair piled high in a cone on his head. A god, but fat and playful. So much more fun than Jesus.

In Java Ganesha's mostly gone underground for obvious reasons, or retreated to a few surviving Hindu villages on mountaintops, along with Hinduism's other thirty-three million gods. Some of these gods are still robustly alive and well in the court dances I saw in the pavilion in Yogyakarta. In fact, so strongly present are these divine figures from the archipelago's ancient Hindu kingdoms that some Muslim clerics in Java have even objected to Muslims taking up classical dancing!

But many do, of course, the Javanese were many things before they were Muslims.

India's a lure for me these days as well (so vast, so infinitely complex, so maddeningly self-contradictory, so polytheistic), but Java is the beautiful enemy I keep my eye on—sigh for, rather than lust for. Java is everything that I am not, at least on the surface, with its fixation on one god in whom I do not believe, its minaretted towns and villages bound by tight webs of social relations based on age-old ideas of family and honour that are wildly foreign, and often hostile, to me. I don't know what India is (to be absolutely honest), India is cloud cuckoo land and a nightmare at the same time, India is foul, unsightly and violent, India is also transportingly beautiful, a Persian miniature of exquisite delicacy, but not my enemy. India has too many faces to be my enemy. India allows me to be whatever I choose, you see, ten times a day. In India I may be occasionally *en garde*, but in Java, from the moment the predawn call to prayer wakes me up, I must spar as deftly as I can with beautiful enemies, perchance (of course) to be seduced.

I stared at my drab mustard-yellow curtains. As I recall, Ganesha's favourite colour was yellow—marigold yellow, to be precise. I don't think Ganesha would like my mustard-yellow curtains at all. I don't like them much myself. Yet, in its own good time, it was in these strangely bland surroundings that my curiosity about the world and how it works had caught fire again, and I felt eager for the sun to come up so I could sally forth and *make* something (even something beautiful) out of the endless chaos surrounding all of us.

Rita's Room Again

Late on the afternoon I arrive back home, Peter and I pad down the corridor to Rita's room at St Ursula's. The moment the main door clicks shut behind us I feel buried alive again, struggling for air. What is this place if not one of Cavafy's yellowish 'small corners', the sort of place you might live out a 'wasted life' in? Rita has never expressed any curiosity about 'harbours hitherto unseen'.

Her door is ajar. Spider-thin under her sheet, she's coming undone.

'Hullo, Rita,' I murmur. 'How are you feeling today?' Peter leans over and kisses her forehead. Her grey hair is so thin, yet it's combed. Somebody has combed it.

She opens her eyes, looks at me with no hint of disquiet, holds out a tremulous blue-veined hand and whispers: 'Olive.'

There can be no ship nor road out of here for Rita, just as there was none for Cavafy's Alexandrian, no other place or 'things elsewhere' to hope for. But has Rita, our Rita, Peter's mother, also 'wasted' her life, like the Alexandrian in the poem, in her small corner of nowhere? Yes and no. It's been an empty life, except on Saturdays. Only one thing—*one thing in all the world*—has been worth staying alive for: her visit every Saturday to see her son. And me and the dog as well, I'm sure. Dog after dog as the years went by. Four dogs. We didn't talk about anything much on all those Saturdays (thirty years of Saturdays), we just cleaned out cupboards, did the ironing, chatted week after week about what was in front of us: a garden bed to be weeded, sardines on toast, the rain, new shoes, the crossword clues—things we could see and hear and touch. She feels things, but never speaks of them. She was throttled early on. She's never read anything apart from *Woman's Day*, not even the books of this much-loved son who is bending to kiss her chalky white forehead, she's never listened to music (not even the Beatles, never mind about Beethoven or Shostakovich)—she's never had curiosity about anything much beyond the front gate, as far as I can tell. Rita has had no inner life to speak of. 'My heart lies buried like something dead,' moans Cavafy's Alexandrian, but he at least dreamt of escape. Rita seems to have dreamt of very little. Kind, she has no heart. She is bored to death.

She loves the touch of Peter's lips, my hand squeezing hers. 'Year after year,' she said once, with a tiny chuckle, 'nobody ever *touches* me.' But she craved it. She still loves to be touched.

We stand the two of us in silence for a moment and look at Rita. The dog finds a patch of sun and lies in it. The smell of cabbage wafts in from the corridor, along with faint whimpers from the room next door. From somewhere across the empty courtyard comes muffled shouting. 'Mngk,' she says, and smiles at us.

Today feels different. Today this good woman we have loved is coming undone. Fragile though she was for many years, she held together, until now Rita has been a self, tightly knit. Now she is unravelling. Today. The 'I' is falling apart before our eyes. How perfectly Sarah Day, who knows Rita well, has put it in that poem of hers ('The Grammar of Undoing' it's called) about her own mother's last days. How did she phrase it? Only a few lines come to the forefront of my thoughts: '... first person singular is out of mind, / is now impossible to find. Where has / the pronoun referring to the speaker gone?' Sentences still have verbs, 'tense, singular and plural all agree', the grammar is still working, but the 'I' has disappeared. But it's not Buddhism, it's dementia.

Even our dog Polly knows that today it's different. Usually she stands a little to one side, allowing a hand to reach out to fondle her, but not looking into Rita's eyes. On this afternoon Polly gazes at Rita, then gets up and walks firmly over to her bedside and lays her head on the sheet close to Rita's face, staring intently into her eyes. Polly is not sad, I don't know what she is, I'm not a dog, but she is not sad. At this instant, which has yawned in the blink of an eye to gobble up the universe, she seems to be seeing *through* to something we cannot see. She doesn't nuzzle Rita's hand, or whine, she just *is* with her, as if holding her together, gently, with her own presence, as best she can, at least, without words, as a dog, for this all-engulfing moment.

'I'll leave you for a moment,' I murmur. I have to go outside, Peter should be alone with his mother. I don't hold with any of this, I don't believe in premonitions or occult transmissions, yet my heart is breaking, swelling inside me at this minute until I'm about to choke, squeezing tears out of my eyes, I am heartsick, that's what I am, there's no other word, this time my heart is sick, it's not grief, we were in friendly cahoots against humbug and loneliness, that's all, we were never close, we shared a love for her son, but farewells rip my heart in two, there is no remedy for last glimpses and final farewells, there have been so many ultimate partings over the years, not a multitude but too many all the same, each one has set up a keening inside me, there was no consolation, the wailing went on and on, silently, and then, in time, the wound would grow over.

Out in the garden behind the Grange amongst the damp mosses, the ferns and azaleas, endings and new beginnings are everywhere you look, in every clump of greenery, every flowerbed, every branch of every tree. The ants, the wrens, the wattle-bird probing for nectar amongst the grevilleas, are all ending and beginning into infinity. Here what I have just seen kaleidoscopes into a new pattern in my mind—unsteadily, and shuddering slightly, it takes its time. I am not consoled, I am shaken, there's a gnawing at my very quick, but at least I can breathe here, I can be stronger.

I don't know what 'love' is supposed to be. I can say it in half a dozen languages, but am still confused. What is it? Do I love Rita? Does Peter? I think she loves us, loves the dog, loves the afternoons in the sun watching us garden or helping me throw things out. She loves throwing things out. At home alone during the week before she fell over all she did was throw things out—blouses, old dinner-sets, shoes, vases, mugs, sheets and rugs. It excited her to empty cupboards, to wipe down the empty shelves, to take the things we were throwing out to the tip, she loved our trips to the tip, her mind quickened at the prospect of the tip. But it is hard (*this must be faced*) to love someone—*love*, not just feel a particular tenderness for or care deeply about—when there is no rich inner life, no *thick* inner life, ballooning here, mushrooming there, to be at one with. No, I don't think I love Rita. I feel a sort of boundless, soft-hearted empathy, there's a bond between us, certainly, after all these Saturdays spent together, as well as gratitude for her kindness, her generosity and acceptance of our many strangenesses, but I don't feel love. I know what loving feels like.

How can I say so confidently, I ask myself, taking the usual damp path around the garden through the ferns and shrubs, that Rita has no inner life (to speak of)? I wince at my own presumption. How would I know? Rita thinks and feels and loves her son, she remembers (if a little blurrily now) her virtually eventless life (father, mother, marriage, a friendship or two, the eventless, long-ago holidays she took in small towns by the sea), she'll look with quickly fading interest at photographs of members of the family doing this or that in black and white, she'll do a crossword almost every morning, flick through a magazine so vapid (royals and recipes) that she can't remember five minutes later whether or not she's even read it, cook a batch of scones, perhaps … but that's not what I mean by an inner life. Still, watching her evaporate like this is unbearable. There are now just droplets of Rita left.

Even Eddy is less effusive today, I find, when I get back to Rita's room. In spotless white as usual, and still on stage, gleaming in the sunlight from the west, but more restrained. He's talking to Peter, even to Polly ('Aren't *you* a gorgeous pooch!'), rather than to Rita, as if she's already left. He brushes back her thin, white hair with his hand, she opens her eyes and smiles. 'Some water, sweetheart? I'll leave it here on the tray.'

'Has she eaten anything at all today?' Peter asks.

'No, we haven't been eating today,' he says, straightening her doona.

Peter pauses and then says to Eddy in a low, flat voice: 'She may not eat again, I suppose.'

'It's unlikely, yes,' Eddy says, gently now, but without a trace of sentiment. He keeps looking steadily at Rita as her eyes slowly close. 'Even if she did eat something, it wouldn't make much difference. Well, none, really.' He swivels and looks at us. 'Do you understand?' We nod. 'I'm sorry,' he says, then leaves us with her. What else could he have said? There's nothing meaningful left for us to say now, and there never will be again.

We sit on for a while in silence. Polly makes a strange, low moaning sound in her throat. Later on, Eddy looks in briefly to check on things and flashes us a smile. 'Sleeping like a baby,' he says, discarding the useless pronoun. We keep sitting. We get up. We kiss her. 'Goodbye, darling,' I murmur. She doesn't stir.

'Goodbye, Mum.'

Happiness and Contentment

When we finally get back to the house, the first thing I do is sit down. I'm home. I've spiralled down into my armchair in giddying, ever-shrinking circles from my far-flung adventures in wilder parts, from those rings of buddhas at the top of the stupa at Borobudur, to the cliff-faces packed with the dead in Sulawesi, whirling round and round, and round and down, swinging out across the sea to Sydney, down to Hobart, over to St Ursula's Grange, then home, to this small blue room, this big blue chair and stillness. In Torajaland home is where your placenta is buried (*tondok lamunan lolo*), which is pretty straightforward, no room there for sentimental waffling, whereas for me home is no longer a place, but something I *do* with Peter and the dog. I could do it almost anywhere.

Prokofiev fills the room. We put on Boris Giltburg with his spidery hands, playing Prokofiev's 8th Sonata at the Queen Elizabeth Hall in London. Boris Giltburg's hands are flying, pounding at the keyboard of the Fazioli in London, dancing on it, prancing on it. (I've watched him on YouTube, I can picture him precisely.) We are transfixed. I feel assailed by Prokofiev's sweet violence, pummelled by it, wildly tossed about by squall after squall of swirling sounds. I really haven't a clue about music, to Peter's chagrin, although I did know Prokofiev's widow in Moscow years ago (very well) and came to his music through her. If I'd had an ounce of musical sophistication, it would presumably have been the other way around. He beguiled me utterly that first winter in Moscow after I'd met Lina Ivanovna, by which I mean that what I heard in the concert halls captured what I felt I was. And so I am in the mood for Prokofiev now—who else?—at this moment of home-coming, and we put him on. He meanders at first, if you remember, in the 8th Sonata, there's a sort of wandering off the track, although the bass line carries you along with him, there's movement, it's never random, and then the storm comes closer, the flurries start, the wind whips up the fragments, wheeling and turning, sometimes even pirouetting with them, soaring, dropping, wheeling, racing, showering us with life-giving clusters, never heard before, not once since time began. You think for a moment you've heard this phrase before, this waltz, this short burst of lyricism, and your heart leaps, but you haven't. It's tumultuous, this sonata, yet intricately patterned, it's introspective and personal early on, yet, written as the sonata was during the war with the Germans, with history breaking through in every note. It's about Prokofiev, in other words, but also about victory over the Germans.

'Why do you like it so much, do you think?' Peter asks quietly, as Giltburg stands (or so I imagine) to acknowledge the thunderous applause. Peter understands music in a way I don't, I'm not intimate with classical music, so he's always pleased to see me swept up by something at a concert or at home in our big blue chairs. I hardly have the words to analyse why I like or love a piece of music—I have words, of course, but a layman's words, I don't really know what a cadence is, let alone a Phrygian cadence or an augmented sixth.

'I like it because *this* is what I mean by an inner life. Pleasure in endless patternings. Rooted pleasure—it must be rooted.'

'Yes.'

'An inner life is a work of art.'

'Yes.'

'It doesn't just sit there, you have to *perform* it.'

As a rule when I first get home from exotic parts, I feel a bit glum and deflated. The first time I ever went away alone (to Western Australia at the age of ten on money I'd won in colouring-in competitions in the Sunday paper), I cried for days when I got back. I was broken-hearted, I think. It was a kind of grief. I'm not sure what I'd lost forever, but I felt the same grief after every trip away for years. On this particular day, though, back from yet another adventure in sultry climes, there is no heaviness of heart at all. In the silence of the small, blue room at the heart of the house, at the age I am, I feel no grief at all. I feel what I feel more and more often now I'm old: a deeply rooted contentment.

Until you reach a certain age, contentment can be

hard to achieve. The Buddhists next door, although they're still in their thirties, do project a certain kind of contentment when they greet you, it's true, the kind people feel when they believe they can see beyond the appalling suffering the world is full of to a higher bliss. Perhaps, like Kartika in Yogyakarta, our neighbours expect nothing. The local vicar often looks cheerful as he passes, but rarely what I'd call *content*. You don't get the impression when you meet him that he's seen through to anything at all quite yet, although by no means has he lost his hope of doing so. The sort of contentment most of my older friends have—and the sort I, too, felt after coming home and listening to Prokofiev's 8th Sonata in my blue recliner—is different. We feel contented (if we are contented) because we have *at last* come to accept that there's not much we can do about the awfulness of everything (the death-dealing violence, the greed, the ecological devastation, the closed minds running the planet)—indeed, at a certain point in our decline, perhaps nothing—and it doesn't matter a jot (to the universe, that is). The letting-go of old myths about the place of human beings in this or any other world, in Bertrand Russell's words, 'brings vigour' to our minds and even to our bodies. It's a life-giving draught in other words, according to Russell, if you can stretch to it, it's an exhilarating lungful of fresh air at a time when life can seem airless.

'Epicurus said much the same thing,' my friend Tim at gay ballroom dancing said when I quoted Bertrand Russell to him during the tea-and-cake break outside, 'but two thousand years earlier. Russell must have got it from Epicurus.' Tim can be a bit competitive. Tim's forte on Friday evenings was the tango, but there was a lot more to tall, thin, bespectacled Tim, it soon transpired, than the tango. Gay ballroom dancing, by the way, is the most exuberantly joyful thing I have ever done in my life. We boys sometimes took the girls' part during the lessons, while the girls played at being boys. We were none of us too pernickety about what our middle fingers or thumbs were doing as we danced, we weren't there to master the art of ballroom dancing, we were there to enjoy ourselves enormously, although we did make some effort to get the footwork right. We rumba'd and cha cha'd, we waltzed and foxtrotted, we jived and tangoed for two hours each week with only one short break for tea and cake. The lesbians brought the cake. As we danced, what was outer and what was inner collided and ignited: spontaneous combustion. The tango in particular makes sparks fly. I would go off like a rocket at the merest hint of 'Jalousie' (which was written by a Dane—who'd have thought?).

It was Tim who first got me to take Epicurus seriously. Until I met Tim, I'd thought Epicureans were just people who ate and drank too much for high-minded reasons—which they often are, but Epicurus himself, as I discovered, was a different kettle of fish entirely. 'Have you ever read anything much about Epicurus?' Tim asked, but he could tell I hadn't. 'You should google him. The trouble is his ideal was a contented, tranquil life, a simple life amongst good friends—with slaves, of course, to keep it simple. But who on Earth wants a happy, tranquil life?' It didn't seem such a bad idea to me at that particular juncture, especially if you were a Greek at the time of Alexander.

'Is "happy" the same as "contented", do you think?'

Tim ate cake for a moment. 'You look as if you're probably contented in general, but actually happy here tonight. As I see it, happiness is something that comes in bursts from outside—love at first sight, winning at chess, getting good news. Happiness is something that seizes *you*. Speaking of which, I was reading the other day about this Russian woman—complicated hyphenated name—who was dying of kidney disease in a clinic in Central Asia after getting out of the gulag. Then suddenly out of the blue news came of the death of Stalin. It struck her like a flash of lightning. In fact, her joy was so overwhelming that she began to get better not by the day, but by the hour! Can you believe it? Kidneys cured by ecstasy. She's now in her eighties and still going … well, not strong, perhaps, but in pretty good fettle for someone who spent all those years in the gulag. You can get her book about it online.' He paused. 'Where was I?'

'Happiness. A line of Shaw's is coming to mind about happiness,' I said, but it never arrived, of course—so many thoughts these days disappear en route. (I've tracked it down. It was a line from *Buoyant Billions*, which Shaw wrote in his early nineties, not long before he died. 'I don't want to be happy,' a character called Mr Secondborn snaps at somebody, 'I want to be alive and active.' I take it Secondborn means that happiness should not be pined for or hunted down, just appreciated when it turns up in the course of an animated existence. I suspect that may be what Tim meant, too, when he said he'd gone off happiness.)

'Contentment strikes me as something much blander than happiness, but more reliable,' Tim went on, straightening his glasses and ignoring my efforts to recall what Mr Secondborn said. 'I think of contentment as an everyday thing. It's what you feel when you don't want anything more—until you do. It's nice, but it needs a shot of happiness now and again.' He examined me from a great height. His height made him a challenge to rhumba with. 'I must say, you look like a fairly contented person to me.'

'Oh, no,' I remember saying, 'I'm not contented at all, believe me. Occasionally I'm happy, though.' Here now, I thought, but didn't say so.

'What makes you happy, then? Have you worked it out yet?'

Before I could think of anything apart from ballroom dancing, a Cuban band (by the sound of it) struck up back inside the hall. Saved by the bell. So we sauntered off, trying to look casually Latin, and got straight into it. The philosophy of happiness would have to wait. This was the real thing.

Old age is a good time to experience contentment, but happiness is harder to come by—as, perhaps, it should be—because happiness has to hit you, as it did Valentina Mikhailovna Mukhina-Petrinskaya on the day Stalin died, like a flash of lightning. You'll be hit by lightning more often, of course, if you put yourself in the way of it—stand beside an open window to watch the roiling clouds gathering, take a walk in a storm now and again. There's no point at all, if you want *happiness*, in adopting a goddess pose and being mindful.

So when Katrine, the old friend who hails from Copenhagen, said to me that what made her happy as much as anything was where she lived, I suspect she was actually talking about contentment. When she goes downstairs and out into the street, she likes the whiff of bohemia that carries on the breeze in that corner of Sydney—nightclub dancers and circus performers amongst the office workers, a few students, professors, old lefties, a ratbag or two, and lots of people who read books. Like most of us, I imagine, she enjoys going to bed and getting up in the morning in friendly territory. It's during the day that you venture into neighbourhoods that are more inhospitable. I know what Katrine means when she focuses on where she lives as a source of 'happiness'. Once upon a time I, too, thought in terms of living somewhere beautiful, perhaps with a water view, or somewhere smart and faintly Swiss where everyone colour-coordinated, read fine fiction and spoke grammatically, but, now I'm no longer young, what makes me feel contented every morning (I rarely leave the house at night, it's too much trouble) when I first look out of the window is the sense that this is where I belong: water rimmed by high green hills backed by a towering violet mountain (it was a childhood fantasy, when I was very small I drew fantasy maps of an ideal city exactly like this one on paper my father had stolen from the office); a comfortably characterful part of the city but with a raffish edge—a poet over the road, artists dotted everywhere, gay activists (the sort that hang out rainbow flags), office workers, students, a few Indians, a Dutchman, three jewellers, two recluses, a baker, a vicar, a dentist, one or two golfers—not all people like me, but people I like to wake up amongst, knowing

I'm welcome, people I can feel empathy for, as they can for me. It's not unlike a large village, and a village is good to be old in.

Is suburban contentment of this kind selfish? If you're going to get Greek about it, as I am increasingly inclined to do, and inch towards some sort of Aristotelian *eudaemonia*, or even towards Epicurean ideas of virtue, you will no doubt come to accept the notion that, without giving thought to the welfare of others, you simply cannot achieve the peace of mind, the easefulness, you seek between explosions of happiness. In other words, to be at peace you must love others as (yes, that's right) yourself. Not the crazy guy around the corner who poisons cats, but others in general. Your tranquillity is no more than an arrangement with your psyche so long as others are suffering, just as friendship is just a pact unless it is based on virtue. Consequently, if we watch the nightly news, let alone talk to our family and friends, our contentment can never be complete. Until the end of the universe, contentment is doomed to incompletion. Even in some remote Bhutanese valley where the outside world and its cataclysms—the Syrias, Brazils, Myanmars and other scenes of violent upheaval—are distant, contentment is bound to be partial.

Happiness, though, can indeed be perfect. Needless to say, it doesn't last, but that's in the nature of things. Love doesn't last, either, as Bertrand Russell pointed out in his musings on happiness, but it can still (if I might borrow images from the Persian poet Hafiz) bejewel your soul or even split you open like a shaft of light. Love, wrote Hafiz, and you will be shot like an arrow into God. It's a Sufic take on things. At least Hafiz didn't try to whirl our small lives away into nothingness, as so many believers do. It was only fear and darkness he wanted to banish from our hearts. I'm very taken with Hafiz.

By the time you reach maturity, you really should know what makes you happy. There's no point in waiting until senescence hits. I don't mean cheerful or pleasantly relaxed, as you might feel sprawled on the sofa with a Josephine Tey, your dog by your side, rain pounding on the window-panes, but positively *happy*. I'm talking about radiance. You should know what triggers the illuminations deep inside you, or at least enlivens you and fires your spirit from top to toe. Robert Louis Stevenson was strongly in favour of knowing: 'To know what you like is the beginning of wisdom and of old-age.' If you're past your prime, you should have a list.

Nobody needs a happiness list in their twenties or thirties, as Stevenson surmised. Having one before you reach forty—an actual, written list on a sticky note or a piece of paper—could be the sign of a compulsive disorder, like praying or sending Christmas cards. Until you're forty you should be constantly experimenting to find out what transports you: playing rugby, group sex, rock-climbing, singing in a choir, origami, downhill skiing, sky-diving, the eucharist, amateur dramatics, poker, trying out new Ottolenghi recipes, flying into Leh airport in northern India (any airport in northern India, for that matter—try going into Gangtok in a helicopter, for instance)—really, the possibilities will be without number. By the time you reach middle age, the list of things that make you happy will no doubt have shrunk, although the pleasure they afford you may well be much sharper. In old age, when stamina is at a premium, you may need to keep your little list by the bed. Your happiness could very well be my contentment, mine your idea of tedium unalloyed—but that's of no consequence whatsoever. Once you get to the final act in the drama, all you need to keep constantly in mind is what makes *you* happy—makes you dance—put yourself in the way of it as often as you can. Wave until it notices you are there. Who cares what the family thinks? You're old. You're never going to get another chance in all eternity.

Happiness, like art, happens when what is seen pierces what is unseen in you and sets fire to it. When this happens you kaleidoscope with a brightness so intense it will dazzle your inner eye. If you have no inner life to speak of, happiness may well remain a mystery to you. Pleasure won't be hard to come by at all, but happiness, in Tim's sense of the word, will be beyond your grasp.

'So why are you not contented?' Tim asked with a small grin as he pulled up outside my house, to drop me off after dancing. 'Often happy, you said you were, but not contented. You look as if you're more or less at ease with yourself.' He had a fine profile against the streetlight. I like strong lines.

'I'm contented in patches, I suppose,' I said, staring out into the suburban blackness. He cut the motor, so I felt I had to say *something*. 'But satisfaction doesn't last, does it. There's always something missing. Must be a hangover from the old idea that everything should add up to something, although it never does. Nor do we. And, to be honest, I'm not sure I'm too concerned about being at ease with myself. For example, I really don't want my chakras balanced. What I want is to be alive.'

Tim said nothing, he just tapped his knee and stared straight ahead at the empty street. Perhaps he set great store by balancing chakras.

'So what makes you happy, then? You were about to tell me, I think, but ...'

'Yes, the salsa music started up.'

'I get the feeling dancing makes you happy.' It was his nose I liked, I think. You can't go past a good Greek nose.

'Any sort of Latin rhythm.'

'Why?'

'It's the combination of playfulness and discipline in

Latin dancing. It's dynamite. It's how I want to live my life.'

'You make it sound like S&M,' he murmured, adjusting his spectacles with one finger. He reached across me to open the glove box, looking for a cigarette. He lit it. 'Or am I wide of the mark?'

Another smackeroo blurdy! At that precise moment I hadn't the faintest idea.

※

In the small hours of the morning, as I slowly floated back down to Earth (I can never fall asleep immediately after the excitement of ballroom dancing), I thought again of Barbara's mother lying 'happily' on her bed in deep old age, her hair a fright, simply reminiscing. Had that really been 'happiness'? At a certain point, when you're 'graveyard-old' (as Liz McQuilkin, a friend of mine, called it in a poem), is this what 'happiness' mostly amounts to: lying on your bed, remembering? Is that as elated as you're going to get? Will happiness finally sink out of sight in a bog of contentment?

The time certainly comes when there's not much

point in picturing the future. The ancient father of a friend of mine doesn't even buy green bananas these days because he doesn't want to waste his money on something he'll never eat. Mind you, even physiologically speaking, imagination is all of a piece: once you can't picture the future, you probably can't remember much about the past, either. So long as the synaptic links are firing, however, and fabrication is one of your strengths, long-term memories can often be retrieved from the wrinkled cerebral mantle even in advanced old age. The time does come when memories linked to the hippocampus (what you just read, what you just watched on television—most of what happened in the last half hour) dry up very quickly. So presumably what Barbara's mother was doing was fossicking around pleasurably in her cerebral cortex rather than the hippocampus.

One of the hopes you nurse in recollecting is that, like a good novel, your life will acquire some sort of narrative thrust as you relive key episodes in it. If only the right connections can be made between all those knots of memories, a pattern will emerge, just as it does in art, you think, even in Malevich's 'Black Square' (which is a comfort). Moving from cluster to cluster—and memories do actually cluster physiologically in the brain—we long for a sense of things being *meant*, being ordered, as they are in any good piece of fiction, even the more satisfying kind of biography. But in reality there are only clusters—lying in ruts all too often, but all the same, only clusters. There's your first headmaster, there's Sister Mary Francis teaching you the scales, there's your wedding in a country church, there's arriving in Moscow, arriving in Casablanca, arriving in Kathmandu, the dog dying. They don't add up to anything at all. Memory is not the movie of your life.

My first memory (just a handful of very faded scraps), for instance, is of being in a train at the age of two, headed with my parents for a holiday by the sea at Boat Harbour, north of Sydney. At some point a tall, thin man in a broad-brimmed hat came up the aisle and I asked him if he was God. He chuckled and said I was exceptionally well-spoken for two. I remember the man in the train, I expect, because I can leap from him to any number of other memory clusters: trains, importuning strangers, looking fruitlessly for God, being good with words, a kind of impudence, being odd. To this day tall, thin men in broad-brimmed hats on trains catch my eye. For all I know now the whole thing is a confabulation, but it's vital to my delusion of having a self. The truth is that recalling all these clusters one by one does not produce a grand narrative—not really, not as such—just more scattered nodes of memory, joined to each other by a tangle of filaments so fine they can easily snap. For the most part, they are a delight to play amongst, slipping from one to another and going absolutely nowhere.

There's no doubt about it: immersing yourself in memories in this way *thickens* the life you're having now. Who wants to live thinly? Bernard Berenson wanted to thicken his life by reliving it in his mind (the mind he once called a 'tapestry') and by rereading books he'd loved over the years. 'A wave of longing' swept over him from time to time, he said, for places he had seen when much younger: from Upsala, he wrote in his diary, forgetting it has two p's, 'to the Sahara, from Gibraltar to the Euphrates … Not only would I see again all I have seen, but read again all that I have enjoyed, all that has fed my spirit … I want to hear again all *die alten Weisen* [the old ways of doing things]. Infinite longing.' This is the reason I've kept diaries of my travels—my own exploits on the banks of the Euphrates, in Sweden, the Sahara, Gibraltar, but also much, much farther afield: to live again as I reread them, to be reborn as a daring adventurer in the middle of a quiet afternoon ensconced in my blue recliner. The diaries are all lined up on a top shelf in my study going back twenty-five years. Over the years they've become much sketchier, less literary, as Edward Said predicted. All the same, half an hour with any one of them is sensationally enlivening.

What I like about Berenson, by the way, for all his Bostonian snobbishness, is his capacity for pleasure, even in his early eighties. 'There is a certain sweetness,' he wrote in his diary for 17 June 1947, 'in being what one is now—not reduced but contracted ...' A tightening takes place, in other words, a compression, as we grow older, lending a particular kind of sweet intensity to the enjoyment of our memories. This idea appeals to me more than Horace's dream of 'enjoying the gentle pleasures of life' in old age. It might depend on what sort of life you've led.

Berenson does not, however, come across in his diaries as obsessed with the narrative arc of his life, as so many of us can become, as if our lives were 'stories' needing a beginning, a climax and a gentle dénouement in prospect. That's not a life, that's a novel. When we take up a novel, we're usually hoping for something— otherwise we'd put the book aside. What is it that we're turning the pages in the hope of? What keeps us caring about what comes next in a tale that's make-believe? (Or 'just made up', as Rita called all fiction, including the fiction her own son writes. Rita never read because she didn't care a jot about what came next *in a work of art*, only in everyday life, and she could get that from the Hobart *Mercury*. Rita did not seem to think abstractly.) At the very least, we're hoping to find out how everything turns out: will the evildoers and ne'er-do-wells be punished and the hero and heroine finally commit adultery? This is the level of art as sheer entertainment, and sometimes sheer joy. At a more complex level we no doubt hope for something more emotionally and intellectually amplifying.

As my friend Suzy puts it, what we crave has something to do with the human heart. We were trying one morning to work out why the latest masterpiece by an acclaimed novelist had bored us both half to death. Vast, passionate, brilliantly written in the kind of English no

English-born writer would dare attempt, it left us both yawning. Neither of us quite finished it (as many, indeed, never finish their lives for much the same reason). When Suzy and I read fiction, above all things we want to learn more about the human heart. Where else can we turn, if not to fiction? To films nowadays, of course, and we do. Interestingly enough, Indonesians call their liver (*hati*) their 'heart' in this sense. It doesn't matter what you call it. The squishy body part is just a metaphor in both languages for the inner life or psyche where feelings, experience and memory mix. A vivid awareness of this vital organ is what keeps us turning the pages, in art and life itself. Once upon a time readers may have hoped for answers to much larger questions while following the intricacies of a love story or even Biggles up the Zambezi: in essence, in the old days, we half expected to be told how to save the planet. Not any more: we have *Four Corners* and David Attenborough for that. Literature isn't up to it. For the most part, though, storytellers throw little light on the human heart. Instead, they all too often chronicle the lives of the sort of people we bump into in the soft-drink aisle at the supermarket. May they all live long and happy lives, but who wants to read about them? Private lives, even the private lives of the good and great, are not necessarily *inner* lives. I want to read about lives that transform mine in unimagined ways, not lives that outwardly mirror mine. Even as a small child I wanted to read books about Iceland, Greenland and Tibet, or at the very least something about William by Richmal Crompton, set in Kent, not books about families like the one next door. What I hope for when I read is transfiguration.

Our own biography is unlikely to sustain us in our less active years, as a more intricately patterned inner life would do. 'Why do I wriggle and toss at the idea of being biographied?' Berenson asked himself in his diary toward the end of his eighty-ninth year, long after his achievements as a scholar and connoisseur of Italian Renaissance painting had made him famous. 'It makes me uncomfortable and unhappy. Is it only because there are so many big and little episodes I wish forgotten? Of course, I have much behind me that I hate to recall ... Every kind of *lâcheté*, meanness, pettiness, cowardice, equivocal business conduct (due more to ignorance and the ethics of art dealers than to my own nature), humiliations, furtiveness, ostrichism, etc ... How passionately one wants to forget!' At the same time, one has already forgotten almost everything one ever did anyway. It's not just what I watched on Netflix last week, either. I have no memory at all, for instance, of ever going to a party. At some point in the last eight decades I must have gone to a party—a New Year's Eve party, a birthday party, a college bash, a jolly gathering of some description with loud music and things to eat and drink. But I have no recollection of ever being at a party at all. The unbearable humiliation that parties gave rise to (over and over again) has been wiped from my memory. If I scrunch up my eyes and say 'party' over and over again to myself, I'll just get the faintest whiff of teenage sweat in my nostrils. It, too, will eventually fade. Indeed, forgetting is as important as remembering to a balanced life—and not only one's hideous *faux pas* and shameful deeds. Nobody takes pleasure in forgetting for pathological reasons—because the medial temporal lobe has gone haywire, for instance, or the cerebral arteries are clogged with plaque—but unless you gradually forget almost everything you'll go mad. To be completely frank, I write partly in order to forget. I am always mildly astonished when readers assume I would be interested to learn more about Venice, Corfu, Ivan Turgenev or any of the other characters and places in books I've written. I am interested in a thousand and one things, but not those. I wrote in order to purge myself of them.

In Berenson's case it seems to have been not chiefly shameful episodes from earlier years that made him wary of being 'biographied'. The whole illusory narrative arc—the telic trajectory—went against the grain.

I dread having my life written as the 'success story', as it is bound to be, seeing that economically and socially I had to make my way from nothing at all. Yes, economically and socially, but I never from the earliest dawn of consciousness felt proletarian or inferior to the highest class anywhere. I never felt that I was climbing, being promoted from an inferior to a higher standard of life, to a higher social class. I felt only that I was coming into my own, what I had always regarded as belonging to me, of which, for no fault of my own, I had been deprived.

Only one thing about remembering gives me joy: the drift towards an inner patterning, despite *everything*, away from the disorder of the body and the outer world. It's a bit like contemporary scriptwriting, really, where so often on the surface it's pure pandemonium, with no coherence of theme or plot at all. Yet, as the writer of *The IT Crowd* sitcom puts it, these shambolic plot elements which don't really 'go together' at all, are nonetheless held together by 'character'. The episode works. The 'characters' remain true, that's the important thing, he says, and whatever happens in a given episode is true to their established 'characters' (the daffy department head who knows nothing about IT, the zany computer genius, the work-shy technical assistant). Character resists the collapse into meaninglessness. I seem to remember Ernest Becker choosing the same word to describe a common ploy to avoid death: 'character'. In the absence of a soul, he wrote, one of the things we do to (fruitlessly) ward off dissolution is create a character for ourselves, often in the image and likeness of our father's.

In the small hours of the morning, while pondering these things, I remember Rita. Even in the last stages of disintegration, at the end of a largely plotless life, Rita still had character. She was Rita and nobody else on

Earth. It gives me heart. And I think to myself in the darkness: *Rita's life may have been of little consequence, but at least she mattered unfailingly to the two people who mattered to her.*

Who Cares?

One intriguing thing Edward Said wrote in those ruminations of his on the artist's late work—or, at least, on Beethoven's style in his Sonata No. 31, composed close to the end when he was completely deaf—is that the work often becomes 'careless'. What exactly did Said mean? Beethoven slapdash? Hardly—repetitive, even 'wayward' at times (another of Said's expressions), but not slipshod.

So 'careless' of what? The rules, says Said, the conventions. Whether it's true of Beethoven's last works or not (and not all musicologists agree with Said's views on Beethoven), I am in no position to judge, but I think he hit some nail or other right on the head. Towards the end of your run, if you've got your wits about you, you may well become impatient with the conventions you grew up with—or quite a few of them at least—and start shucking them off. You'll know a freedom, if you're growing old well, of a kind you've never enjoyed before in your life. At a certain point towards the end, if you have all your faculties intact, you're unlikely to give a rat's arse about anything very much at all (except, just possibly, global warming). Why is this?

According to the immensely civilised Diana Athill, you don't care about a widening range of things when you're older because your self-esteem is stable—whether low and stable or high and stable, it's stable. You don't need to make choices (to like opera, for instance, or to give a fig who Bourdieu or Beckett or Bradman were) in order to be well-thought-of any more. Until you're well into middle age, your self-esteem is constantly being threatened, you are forever wondering whether or not you are measuring up, or whether you should care about the fact that you obviously aren't. Was it not Bourdieu himself who once said that it was how we think others see us—their *'regard'*—that 'motivates' human action? Some pack animals (which is what we are, after all—animals that live and hunt in packs) do have to keep a watchful eye on their position in the pack, that's true: if hyenas don't keep their wits about them, concealing their infirmities, the other hyenas might gang up on them and tear their throats out. In most civilised human communities, however, this is not a factor. The American celebrity columnist Ann Landers put it succinctly: at age twenty, she wrote, we worry about what others think of us, at age forty, we don't care what they think of us, while at age sixty, we discover they haven't been thinking of us at all. Ann Landers was called a 'boring old biddy' by Ned Flanders on *The Simpsons* after he'd drunk a blackberry schnapps for the first time in his life, and, indeed, her views on marriage were pure drivel, but I find this particular remark of hers astute and liberating. Nobody cares if you're keeping to the rules or not. They never did care if you were keeping to the rules. Not even (probably) your own mother cares if you're keeping to the rules. Apart from your mother and those with a vested interest of some description, nobody is even thinking about you at all. So take a deep breath and rejoice!

The whole subject of what matters in later life and what doesn't came up in a conversation I had recently with Katrine, the Danish friend of mine, who lives in a part of Sydney I'd never have ventured into as a child, although now it's within an inch of being smart. Katrine must be at least eighty, strong-minded and unhampered by received opinion, although she was a little wobbly the day we lunched, having just had a knee replaced. Katrine is not small-boned and usually looks far from fragile. Leafing through that morning's newspaper while waiting for her, I'd chanced upon an eye-catching headline: IT'S LIBERATING TO ADMIT NAOMI WOLF WAS RUBBISH ALL ALONG.

'Look at this,' I said, once we'd grabbed a table, 'it gladdens the heart. Not because it's Naomi Wolf, but because she's saying what she thinks—at last.'

'Who is it?'

'Julie Birchill. The English feminist. Militant, it says here.'

'I know who Julie Birchill is.'

'She's about to turn sixty.'

'Sixty! A wonderful decade, your sixties,' said Katrine, looking strikingly Danish in the minimalist surroundings of the café. 'And turning seventy, in my experience, was even better. My seventies—you're not going to believe this—were one of the best chapters of my life.'

'Really?' I wasn't sure that I could say that. 'Why? What made them so special?'

She thought for a moment, considering the three-legged dog snoozing on the terrace. 'Because I don't have to worry about missing out on anything any more. Does that make sense? I don't care how much you loved the latest Tim Winton—it may well have changed your life, but I just don't want to read it. Lend it to someone else. I don't care who's going to be at the play reading on Sunday—Geoffrey Rush, Judy Davis, who cares?—I just don't want to go, count me out. And also because I don't have to put up with bullshit any more. If I think it's bullshit, I can say so, just like Julie Birchill. So liberating. It puts a smile on my face every day.'

I grinned to hear her enjoying her life so much. 'I wish I were as plucky as you are. I think Samuel Beckett is teeth-grindingly boring, but I'd be careful about where I said it.'

'Just say it. What does it matter if nobody agrees? It doesn't.'

'Well, not much does matter deeply now, I suppose,

at least in terms of the narrative of my own life. The trouble is, if you say precisely what you think about everything, someone will take offence. Take Anzac Day, for instance, or religion …'

'Too bad! Best not to say what you think in *order* to give offence, obviously, not if you're nice, as we are. Whatever you say, though, someone will feel offended.'

'On that question, I rather side with the Stoics. The Stoics held that offence has to be taken, it can't just be given, so we should try not to take it in the first place.'

Katrine thought this sounded admirable, but impractical at the present historical moment. And so, in a Late Style sort of way, we chatted about caring and not caring what people thought for a while—somewhat incoherently, repeating ourselves, quite open-endedly, mostly for the pleasure of the form (chatting)—over the seafood chowder and, in Katrine's case, the pork noodle stir-fry, which smelt mouth-tinglingly good. 'Help yourself to some,' she said.

'I can't,' I said. 'You know—the meat thing.'

'Nobody can see and I won't tell.'

That sounded like Java. What sprang immediately into my mind was the scene on a Garuda flight I'd taken to Flores during Ramadan. Soon after take-off the cabin crew had apologised to the fasting Muslim passengers for being obliged to offer lunch-packs since it was a midday flight. Yet everyone had taken a lunch-pack; the women wearing head-scarves, the men wearing skullcaps, my Muslim companion, Ahmad, on the flight, everyone. Nobody went without their free lunch.

'Should you really be eating that?' I asked Ahmad.

'Why not?'

'Because it's Ramadan and the sun's still up.'

'Nobody can see,' he said, with a grin. I suppose he meant nobody who knew him.

'Can't God see?'

'Who can say?'

The point was that it was not shameful to break the fast since his honour and self-esteem were not at stake amongst strangers and that was what mattered. Nobody cared about the act of breaking the fast, they cared about what people would think of them if they broke the fast. What God was thinking was unknowable. So just have lunch. Most Christians (even Danes these days) come from guilt cultures, however, not shame cultures. In our eyes, what we do is either right or wrong, regardless of who's looking.

Katrine was still waiting to see if I'd like a taste of her stir-fry. 'Just the tiniest bit, then,' I said, affecting to opt for the middle way. 'Mmm, very tasty, I must say.' But wrong—eating animals is wrong. Late in life, though, the need to be always right becomes less pressing than it used to be. When I was in my twenties I was on truth patrol twenty-four hours a day, constantly on the lookout for error—the wrong words, the wrong attitudes, the wrong behaviour. It looks possible when you are young that your own particular notions of right and wrong will eventually hold sway in the world, with the majority of those who disagree with you finally admitting that you were right all along. In the leftish magazines and newspapers I buy, the journalists are still on frantic alert for heresy. On television every day I still see the young, and even the not so young, patrolling the ideological perimeters, weapons cocked, on the lookout for transgressors. In their favourite areas of race, gender and the treatment of disadvantaged minorities they will brook no resistance. Above all, it's the disadvantaged minorities they have strong views on. When disadvantaged minorities, or at least minorities who feel disadvantaged, are exploited or affronted, whole swathes of the younger population become incensed (understandably) on their behalf. Some disadvantaged minorities, however, loathe and detest other disadvantaged minorities, as I know all too well, being a member of a couple, so it's a tangle, but you can usually maintain your rage on a case by case basis if you want to: in favour of the hijab for women today, against binary definitions of gender tomorrow. In old age, you might still care deeply about some of these matters, but probably much less fiercely than you once did and more selectively. If you've travelled beyond your own shores, it will have struck you that the world is irremediably various, the vast majority of intelligent, educated people across the planet disagreeing with you about almost everything with no change in sight. It will have long since dawned on you that your values and opinions will never hold sway anywhere—not in Java or Egypt or Spain, obviously, but not even in Denmark. Your quaint little *Weltanschauung*, however sincerely held, is of no account. And it matters little. All at once, time looks short and largely given over to maintenance: Pilates classes, knee-replacements, endless blood tests, crowns and visits to the podiatrist. Everything else will have to wait its turn.

'What happens, I think,' said Katrine, when I wondered aloud over the coffee why this was, 'is that as you grow older everything shrinks.' She waited for me to react, but I sat chewing this over. 'Your horizons shrink, they narrow sharply.'

I thought of Rita, whose horizons had never been broad but had now shrunk to her bed. 'For example?' I asked.

'Well, when I was younger, I was curious about everything—I wanted to experience everything, go everywhere—to Chile, I remember, for example, that was the place to go at the time, to Timbuktu, to cross the Sahara, to go camping in the Kimberleys, to join a commune—everything was interesting. You had wide horizons, you spread out, you took up causes. I don't have the stamina for that sort of thing any more. Now I have much narrower horizons, but I go deep. It's smaller things that give me pleasure now—conversations with friends about what they're up to or the books we've been reading, extraordinarily intense conversations sometimes with people I meet in the park while I'm walking the dog—with an anaesthetist this morning, for instance, about what consciousness is. I notice my own surroundings in much finer detail than I used to, too: every leaf on the plants in the pots on my balcony, the cockatoos and the rosellas in the park, who's walking better today, whose arm's in a sling, who's having a baby, the clouds, the smells, *everything* ...'

'You've become a miniaturist!' I chipped in. 'It sounds familiar. And at the same time other things recede, don't they. I find I particularly don't care any more about who wins things—the Booker Prize or the Melbourne Cup—do you find that? Or about the royal family, either, and whether or not it's having another *annus horribilis*, or about sending spaceships to Mars, although I do like that whatshisname ... the one with the floppy hair, Brian Cox. It's not the universe I'm so interested in now, really, it's Brian Cox. The universe can look after itself.'

'You feel things acutely, don't you, there are things you desperately want to understand, but it's a much narrower field of things.'

'Well, take Indonesian,' I said. 'Once upon a time when I learnt a language I aimed for perfection, I was ravenous for French, I wanted more and more French, and then more and more Russian. Now I've cast them adrift, I'm learning Indonesian—'

'Are you really? Whatever for?'

'For the pure pleasure of it, for the bizarreness of it, the utter outlandishness of it, the complete uselessness of everything I learn so avidly. But my point is that I don't have to master it. I lock myself up with it in a chair by the window, just it and me, several times a week, and enjoy its company. I'm flirting with it, not possessing it. I'm not going anywhere with it. I know I'll never speak it like a native, even on my good days I limp along in it, mouthing clichés about the weather, but I don't *care*! It's pointless yet profoundly satisfying. It's an adventure every time I try to get my tongue around it, but it's leading nowhere. Exactly like my life.' I paused and studied Katrine's Danish face. 'Actually, I can tell you why I like it because I came up with the word for it last night in bed: I'm refracted by it anew every time I plunge into it.'

'Refracted! Interesting. Is this the first time you've thought of that?'

'All I mean is that, at this late point in my life, I'm

fired up by far fewer things as you are, I try to keep up with very little, but somehow, in these few things that enthuse me, I see a thousand other things. I go down and down and down, not out.'

'Well, you don't take yourself so seriously any more, do you. You take things and people seriously, of course—melting icebergs, homelessness, your grandchildren, but not yourself—not, at least, if you've got any sense.'

'That ex-prime minister who collects clocks—or is it celadon?—always looks as if he still takes himself terribly seriously. Have you noticed? Old radio hosts on their last legs take themselves terribly seriously, too, as do Rear Admirals and Major Generals. Impossible for them to admit that they just don't matter any more, except to close friends—if they have any—and that any mattering they ever did has been almost all forgotten.'

'The thing is you don't have to fix things any more, do you. Or at least I don't. I used to, I remember. Capitalism, for instance, the scandal of church schools, overfishing. It's such a relief not to feel I have to. The world was a circus when I came into it, it still is a circus and always will be.'

'The broader world, you mean.'

'Yes. I still fix *small* things, don't you? Have my teeth looked at, put the bins out and so on, despite the butcher's picnic going on around me. When I was young, around the time we first met, I remember thinking that by the time I was old the Catholic Church would surely have disappeared. When I was indeed finally old, I was dismayed to find that it hadn't. How could that be? Twenty years later I couldn't care less whether it has or it hasn't. So long as someone is carrying on the good work of dismantling it. From *my* neck, however, the yoke has been lifted. No more yokes for me.'

'I still feel passionate about the environment and what's been done to it,' said Katrine. 'As a matter of fact, I'm going to go to that climate change march tomorrow.'

'On crutches?'

'No, I'll just shout from the sidelines.'

Good for Katrine! The number of causes I'd turn up to a march for these days is very small.

Walking back to the railway station later, through the lively, sun-lit inner-city streets that were once so blighted, I reflected that the people in Katrine's part of the city clearly cared about all sorts of things. The bodies and faces I passed were full of purpose, they had ongoing projects, they were conscious of how they looked, yet not quite *soigné*, not harbourside—these streets weren't quite chic yet, the soaring apartment blocks that lined them being far too new and hard-edged to have much class.

I could only guess at what the passers-by here cared about: China, perhaps, or their children, their finances, shopping, food, Jesus, gay rights, child abuse, the South Sydney Rabbitohs, sex, Taylor Swift, immigration, the ivory trade … You could tell from the way they strode along the pavement, got in and out of cars and greeted people they knew that there were things they definitely hoped to fix, as well as things, and possibly people, that they cared about. Things mattered to them in a way they didn't any more to Katrine or me (not to mention Rita), and never will again.

It's a delicate matter to bring up, but an important skill as you age, I think, is knowing when to give up. Nothing could be more fatuous, it seems to me, than the call in Dylan Thomas's villanelle not to 'go gentle into that good night'. Why not? Why rage? Go gentle! It's not a 'good night', of course, it's nothingness, but even so: raging and vowing to live life to the full until the last flash of consciousness is absurd. The American mantra about never giving up (so Dale Carnegie, so Jesse Jackson) just sounds jejune to me these days. Why not give up? (Not everything all at once, that goes without saying.) Everything is not possible, despite the rumours. What a relief! The Kenyan runner Eliud Kipchoge, the first man to run the marathon in under two hours, declared emotionally, just moments after crossing the finishing line in Vienna, that 'no human is limited'. But we are, Eliud, all of us, and it doesn't matter.

If you still crave to climb Mt Everest on crutches, climb it, but giving up the struggle gradually, hope by hope, seems sensible to me, even a comfort, a liberation from anxiety, at a point in life you will recognise when you reach it. In *Fruits of the Earth*, his astonishing hymn to desire, written before he was thirty, Gide urges his reader to turn his desire into 'simply a welcoming' of everything that comes to him. 'Desire only what comes to you,' he writes, 'desire only what you have.' At that point Gide believed what came to you might include God in His totality, but most of us, especially later in life, are likely to lower our sights.

I doubt much came to Barbara's mother Nancy when

she reached her mid-nineties, except memories, and so little by little she, too, eventually gave up longing for things and just welcomed her memories. Still living at home alone, she all of a sudden stopped 'taking any trouble over herself', as we said in those days—in other words, making any effort to look her best. Barbara would find her just lying happily on her bed, not in a geriatric stupor, but smiling, thinking and dreaming, in mismatched clothes with her hair a fright. Up until this point she'd been meticulous about having her hair coloured and styled, choosing her jewellery to match her clothes, applying her lipstick with care. To go out now, Barbara had to coax her to put on a fresh blouse or cardigan. Half the time she didn't even bother to put her teeth in. She said she was happy to just remember, to draw strength, as I would think of it, from the play of the inner self. The shrinking was taking its time, but inch by inch she was finally closing in on herself. You do.

Interestingly enough, Rita took great care with her appearance right up until the day she first fell over and was taken away in the ambulance, never to go home again. Cardigans went with shoes, slacks went with neck-scarves, eyebrows were trimmed, her hair was carefully cut and styled. She didn't care about much else (famines in Africa, for instance, or Aboriginal health), but she did make a point of caring about how she looked.

You have to care about *someone*, of course, until the end. Issues fade along with causes, and whether or not the shed needs clearing out becomes immaterial, but you do care about *someone*—your spouse, your beloved friends, your grandchildren, your mother, your cat, *someone*. If you care about nobody, then you will be lonely as the years pass. For example, Rita. Peter and I had cared about Rita. When the call from St Ursula's came late one evening, startling us in our blue recliners, and we knew she was no more, the emptiness we both felt was all-engulfing. It had not so much been love attaching us to her, however, as caring. It had been what my friends in Yogyakarta called *kasih sayang*, a deep affection you ache with a little. (This is the sort of thing you have to get exactly right in Javanese society.) It had been, in other words, a kind of caring tenderness, we had held her firmly in our hearts.

An hour or two with a woman like Katrine reconfigures all the shards in my life—the dull ones, the bright ones, the jagged ones, the ones I'd never noticed before. I enjoyed the walk back to the station through the spruced-up streets of South Sydney. I felt exhilarated. I felt primed for whatever might happen next. Walking, I decided, is really a kind of dancing.

The Dance in Yogyakarta

On the last visit I made to Yogyakarta, I went one evening to watch some children dance. Barbara had suggested it, she knows about these things. It was supposed to be a birthday treat to myself, but by the time the taxi arrived to take me into town, the whole hotel knew it was my birthday. From the point of view of the gardeners and the room-boys, the waitresses and reception staff, I was almost infinitely old, like some ancient king in a fairytale. The cook made me a birthday cake, and everyone gathered in the foyer, smiling, to sing 'Happy Birthday', but before I could eat a single mouthful, the taxi drew up at the door, Barbara waving from the back seat, and off we sailed into the twilight. I never saw the cake again.

Who would have imagined that a dozen Javanese boys and girls learning classical court dancing could crystallise for me the essentials of the art of growing old? Not some bearded Greek philosopher or Himalayan guru, as you might expect, but a group of local teenagers intent on mastering an elaborate ancient art. As a rule youngsters fail to engage me: I scarcely notice they're there, even if they live next door, more focused as I am on adults and animals. On the particular Monday evening I have in mind, however, in a secluded pavilion near the Sultan's palace, I noticed.

The pavilion, or traditional open-sided *pendopo*, where all this happened is hidden in behind the garish, ramshackle shopfronts on Brigadir Jenderal Katamso Street (through a white gateway, past a colonnaded market, deserted at that hour, but still smelling faintly of rotting fruit). It wasn't what I'd expected at all, although Barbara had been there several times and told me about it. It was a wanly lit cluster of white pillars under a high, pinched *joglo* roof. In these shabby, smelly, potholed backstreets, within earshot of the crashing cacophony out on the main road (the roaring, squawking, screeching, thumping din of inner Yogyakarta just after nightfall), it was exquisite, dreamlike, floating there in the blackness on the murmur of unseen flutes and lutes and finely tuned gongs. It looked as if at any moment it might vanish. For the first few minutes Barbara and I just stood where the taxi had dropped us and stared at it in silence.

There was almost nobody there at that hour in the early evening—just the dancing-master (a slip of a man) with two boys on the gleaming tiled platform in the middle of the *pendopo*. Slowly, with studied grace, the three of them were executing an ancient male court dance. Like mating birds, yet not exactly birds. So lethally refined, beyond masculine. Like shadow puppets on their rods, it seemed, feet barely touching the ground. Rocking, loose-kneed. Every fingertip and toe, every eyelash, delicately (but not daintily) angled.

All three were wearing T-shirts and jeans—it was just a rehearsal, after all—with a long, brilliantly coloured scarf, or *sampur*, draped over their shoulders (lilac, midnight blue, canary yellow). Now and again, with their left hand, they'd flick it, quick as a blink. There was no gamelan orchestra, just a small speaker.

Yet all the same, something timeless was conjured up by these three figures, teacher and pupils. They were skewing time as we watched. They were themselves, of course—Lantip, Roso, Midi—yet at the same instant countless others as well, alive again all of a sudden, or still alive, through them.

When the music stopped, and the teacher began talking quietly to his pupils, I turned to Barbara and whispered: 'The boy in red ...'—and she half-turned to me in the shadows where we sat to one side—'... is a bit too plump for this sort of thing, don't you think?' After all, as Barbara was aware (having intricate knowledge of these things), these boys were training to kill (as it were) with deadly grace; there was no room for stockiness. Their movements embodied an introspective, contained radiance, if I can put it like that, but still, their grace was meant to be martial. It was restraint in the face of tumult.

Barbara smiled. 'He's still very young, I suppose,' she said. 'Fourteen? Fifteen? There's still time.'

'I like the other one—the one with the yellow scarf. I like ...'

'Yes,' she said, with a chuckle, 'I imagine you do. The way he stretches out his leg like …'

'… a flamingo.'

'A flamingo? But the knee …'

'Or an ibis, say. A wading bird, at any rate. About to take flight. Slim legs, delicate. But I like the way he does everything.' Nobody (I wanted to say but couldn't quite put it into words) is male *like that* where you and I come from. 'His movements are completely masculine, there's nothing limp about them, yet at the same time …'

'*Halus*,' she said softly. 'Refined, smooth. What they are is called *halus*.' Well, whatever it's called, between Java and the South Pole nobody knows how to do it. Where I live, manly means something brawnier, a manly man is more of a blade. The Javanese have doughty and dashing as well, of course—they call it *gagah*. Later in the evening the smooth and subtle teacher was superbly *gagah* himself: head up, with thrusting legs and a *quick* face—how else can I put it? But at least the Indonesians can choose.

Some young girls arrived in the parking lot beside the pavilion in dazzling sarongs and *kebayas*. When the dancing-master nodded to them, they drifted elegantly across the honey-coloured tiles onto the platform. Where I live, women are usually dressed in black, of course. In the Sultanate of Yogyakarta women everywhere, all kinds of women, women wearing *jilbabs* (as they call the hijab here), teenagers, little girls, grandmothers, all of them play with colour. Here, for all the filth, the derelict buildings, the rubbish-strewn verges, the utter destitution of so many people, women splash the world with colour. As the girls took up position and the gamelan music started up again, the plump boy in red and the slimmer boy in the yellow scarf squatted in the half-light beside the glistening tiled platform to watch.

For the next half-hour or so these girls, with the deliberate serenity of a Javanese women's palace dance, their faces expressionless—or demure, perhaps, or chaste or unassuming, but not, I think, timid—entranced us with their precisely synchronised steps and gestures. This was not Bali, you see, this was Java, so there was no hint of flashiness. Beneath the sleekness, the silkiness, the performed serenity of every movement, there must lie, you knew, century upon century of schooling—yes, of culture, if you like, but 'culture' is such a tired word now. This schooling in self-knowledge has its roots in what surrounds and embraces you rather than in what makes you stand out. At that instant we were watching not just a dance-lesson, but schooling, going back to India, to Hindustan, and to whatever came before Hindustan. The Greeks? Apparently, some scholars discern an ancient connection to Alexander and *The Iliad*. Indian archaeologists, I saw in the paper recently, are suggesting it might even all have begun with the gods themselves. I doubt that, but who am I to say?

However deep the roots, we were observing a lesson in a particular kind of self-understanding. The dancing was clearly an enactment of some kind of self-understanding, although not in a Western self-realisation or heightened self-awareness sense at all. Instead, the self in these dances is an instance of refined abundance.

It was spine-tingling, I was spellbound. Clock-time had melted. Then Barbara, back in clock-time (and peacock green, by the way, or was it more an emerald? I've certainly never seen Barbara in black) suggested a bowl of meatballs and noodles from the street vendor who had set himself up with his steaming cart out in the courtyard. Although a vegetarian (with an admitted weakness for crispy duck), I was utterly transported at that moment and having begun to lose my bearings, I said yes.

As we sat and ate (it was delicious), waiting at the back of the pavilion near the old puppet theatre for the teacher Lantip to join us, I was all at once aware that in watching children learn to dance in this old *pendopo* in Yogyakarta I, too, was learning something, something that had nothing to do with Javanese court dancing, yet mirrored it. These children and their teacher had unwittingly *performed* answers to the age-old question that has been constantly in my thoughts: how to live through to old age *well*, taking pleasure in what we have, given tolerably good health and a sound mind. That's how Horace asked the question, for instance, in a celebrated ode to Apollo, dreaming of an old age that has a knowing, even stylish grip on itself, 'given good health and a sound mind'. But he had no clear answers.

Over the months since Rita fell and sickened, I have pictured the key to living into old age well (living well at any age, really, but particularly towards the end when the body is infirm) as an inner life. But how to shape it? In Java and the surrounding islands the shaping happens when the seen and the unseen mix. In Bali, for instance, the dancer unwraps and then stares at a mask, allowing its force to enter him and shape his steps. In South Sulawesi, too, the dancer opens a window to let 'the spirits' dance into him and open him up to acting out what 'humanises' both him and those watching. But I am not from these islands, I am a Westerner, my thinking springs from the Enlightenment, 'spirits' don't enter the equation, and I have to imagine what happens differently. Wordlessly, with childlike seriousness, these children learning to dance had danced it. And children are somehow of the essence here—not having children necessarily, but being childlike. Perhaps you have to be an outsider, as I was in that pavilion, for this sort of thing to happen to you in a flash like that. Not belonging brings you alive, eyes wide open, it wakes up your imagination, it quickens you.

An abundant inner life that sustains us right through to the end is something that *happens* when we open up to what surrounds us and then dance it, speak it, write it, sing it, love it, turn it upside down and inside out behind our eyes, it's not something that just lies there like gallstones. It is shaped by an unending, playful curiosity about the world, obviously, and by upsurges of creativity and swirls of conversation, but *rooted* curiosity, creativity, conversation, as the children's dancing is rooted in the *Ramayana*. The trick as always is to be playful and schooled at the same time—in anything, by the way, from stamp-collecting to Sanskrit grammar, that opens the door to the particular infinite enfilade of rooms that you will take most pleasure in performing your life in, one after the other. Then, I'm inclined to believe, in Bernard Berenson's wise words, you will discover there is 'a certain sweetness in being what one is now—not reduced, but contracted—so appreciative, so enjoying, so grateful for what has been, and for what is now. It means something to be able to rise above aches and pains, and inertias, and to glory in the world as displayed to one's experienced senses and ordered mind.'

After slurping down our *bakso* broth, Barbara and I took our seats at the back of the pavilion again, wondering if the lesson was over or not. The plumpish boy in red was sitting cross-legged on the floor nearby. '*Selamat malam*,' I murmured with a little smile.

'Hi,' he said in English, as the gamelan music started up again. 'I hope you like.' As poised as a courtier.

'I don't want it to end! How long have you been learning classical dance?'

'Ten years now.' So he wasn't fourteen. Seventeen, perhaps. You just can't tell in Java.

'So why do you learn?'

He didn't hesitate. 'I do it for my soul,' he said.

It was a perfect moment.

Acknowledgements

In conversations about ageing in three or four countries while I was writing this book, these friends shared experiences and thoughts I found particularly illuminating, and I am grateful:

Barbara Hatley
Isabel Huggan
Jennifer Lindsay
Susan Varga
Drusilla Modjeska
Kirsten Garrett
Di Morrissey
Kartika Affandi
Phil Ladlow
Katharina Retsch
Peter Timms

These friends of mine do not in all cases appear in these pages under their own names, nor are our conversations reported word for word. They have been reworked to form a more coherent picture.

The hotel south of Yogyakarta is d'Omah Hotel, Tembi.

I am grateful to Sarah Day for permission to reproduce her poem 'The Grammar of Undoing' from her collection *Towards Light and Other Poems* (Puncher and Wattman, Sydney, 2018).